The
 BLACK
NOTEBOOKS

Other Books of Poetry by Toi Derricotte

Tender
Captivity
Natural Birth
The Empress of the Death House

The ❧BLACK NOTEBOOKS

An Interior Journey ❧

Toi Derricotte

W. W. NORTON & COMPANY

New York   London

Copyright © 1997 by Toi Derricotte

All rights reserved
Printed in the United States of America
First Edition

For information about permission to reproduce selections
from this book, write to Permissions, W. W. Norton &
Company, Inc., 500 Fifth Avenue, New York, NY 10110.

The text of this book is composed in ITC Veljovic Book with
the display set in ITC Veljovic Bold.
Composition by A. W. Bennett, Inc.
Manufacturing by The Maple-Vail Book Manufacturing Group.
Book design by Charlotte Staub.

Library of Congress Cataloging-in-Publication Data

Derricotte, Toi, 1941–
      The black notebooks / Toi Derricotte.
          p.   cm.
      ISBN 0-393-04544-7
      1. Derricotte, Toi, 1941–   —Notebooks, sketchbooks, etc.
   2. Afro-American women poets—20th century—Biography.
   3. Afro-Americans—Social conditions—1975–   4. Race
   awareness—United States.   5. Race relations—United
   States.   I. Title.
   PS3554.E73Z464   1997
   818'.5403—dc21
   [B]   97-5855
                                                                      CIP

W. W. Norton & Company, Inc.
500 Fifth Avenue, New York, N.Y. 10110
http://www.wwnorton.com

W. W. Norton & Company Ltd.
10 Coptic Street, London WC1A 1PU

1 2 3 4 5 6 7 8 9 0

To Bruce
and in
Memory of
Audre Lorde

Contents

If you bring forth what is within you,
what is within you will save you.
If you do not bring forth what is within you,
what is within you will destroy you.

Jesus, in the Gnostic Gospels

Introduction:
Writing *The*
Black Notebooks

Language is the only homeland.
CZESLAW MILOSZ

I began writing this book in the middle of a severe depression. My husband and I had just moved into an all-white middle- and upper-class neighborhood ten miles from New York City. I had spent months looking at houses, over eighty, and I had decided not to take my husband with me to the real estate offices because when I had, since he is recognizably black, we had been shown houses in entirely different neighborhoods, mostly all-black. I had soon found that houses in the "best" neighborhoods, perhaps like the produce and meat in the "best" supermarkets, are comparatively less expensive. At night, under cover of darkness, I would take him back to circle the houses that I had seen and I would describe the insides.

I am the kind of person who can cut her finger in a serious way, or bruise or burn myself badly, and not remember how or when it was done. I have trained myself in a very distinct way of forgetting. Living in a neighborhood in which I was inescapably weighted and bound by race, in which I was the known "black" person, felt entirely different from my previous experience in the white world, a world in which I am usually invisible. My husband says that most black people learn they can't escape from their skin in childhood. I didn't learn it until then.

I began to be conscious that my reaction to hearing a comment in a shoe store or seeing a young black boy on the street was a reaction of fear. My adrenaline would increase, the fight-or-flight response, as if a part of me wanted to jump out of my skin. A dark man who had been a marine told me how, after six weeks of boot camp during which time he wasn't allowed to look in a mirror, he came upon himself in an uncovered mirror and was filled with dread and sadness. He had forgotten he was black.

I wanted to get away, not only from that black person who seemed to be the catalyst of my feelings, but, more to the point, to get out of my own mind, from those thoughts and feelings I so loathed in myself. My reactions were not rational, not "thought." They seemed to be as visceral as instinct. James Baldwin said, "The white man needs the nigger because he cannot tolerate the nigger in himself." But does the black man, too, need the nigger? I sensed that the structures that hold us together as a society and create devastating realities may be built around the most basic instincts for self-preservation.

These structures must originate even before conscious memory, because I truly cannot remember the first time I "learned" I was black. It is as if every experience I have had of realizing I am black, all the way back to grade school and before, when I used to wander undetected across Conant Avenue to where the Polish people lived, is tainted with that fear of discovery, of being recognized as black.

So many black people spoke of hatred for "them," for those "niggers" who were messing it up for the rest of us. It *is* self-hating and destructive, but racism *is* insane, and, surviving it, we have often had to think in desperate ways. "Forget" sounds like such a passive act, but anyone who has experienced the powerful force of repression will know the effort it takes to unforget, to remember.

I began to be aware of that state of consciousness that so alarmed me, that "remembering" of myself as a black person. I began to keep track of it, to write of it in my journals. I believed that my unconsciousness of my blackness, my "forgetting," was symptomatic of some deep refusal of "self," a kind of death wish, and I felt that my symptoms, however much I was alarmed by them, carried some real and essential message that, once acknowledged, I could eventually accept and understand. Of course, these writings were private. I told no one. I was especially afraid that other blacks would discover my shameful feelings. My writing was an expiation, a penance. It was a way I gained distance and control. It was finally a way to transform what I hated and denied into something beautiful and true. Ironically, it became the way I took on, publicly and irrevocably, the very identity I was ambivalent about.

I didn't do this out of desire; desire would never be enough to sustain such explorations. I did it to save my life.

Shame has been a difficult emotion to acknowledge in our experience as blacks, difficult to name, to deal with—as if, if we talk about shame, we will indeed be shameful. For that reason, I have struggled many years to write and publish this work.

I am speaking for myself. Something inside me has guided me to write about my shame, something that knows that wherever there is repression and silencing of the self, there is also the killing oppression. If there are others who have felt that electricity in the heart, I hope I speak for a part that needs release, understanding, and acceptance.

Many readers want literature that concentrates on solutions, on the strength and survival aspects of being black. The benefit is, of course, to nourish those of us who are starved for "positive" images, for images of power. However, might these "hopeful" images defend against knowledge of racism's most devastating, deep-rooted, and intransigent blows, giving false assurance that the effects of racism are not universally devastating?

What are the reasons for the silence that exists about internalized racism, for the lack of personal admissions? We are afraid we will be criticized. We are afraid to know the ways in which the people closest to us, our parents, relatives, and friends, have contributed to our shames, fears, inadequacies, hatreds, and repulsions.

I wanted not to invent and capture the language of hope, which I felt had never been really truthful, faced the worst, or given us an answer, but wanted to record the language of self-hate, which I hoped would take us deeper.

People have asked why my parents, grandparents, and I never "passed" over into the white world. It was unthinkable. With my dark grandfather driving, my grandmother and I would ride in the backseat of my grandfather's Cadillac as if we were being chauffeured. We'd shop the aisles at Saks Fifth Avenue when there wasn't even a black elevator operator. On the one hand, there was always a feeling of anxiety that something would betray what we really were; on the other, I think we were really quite self-possessed, almost arrogant. We saw ourselves, with all of our struggles and complexities, as rich in culture and history, fierce, determined, strong, and even beautiful. While we wanted the privileges white people had, we had contempt for what we saw as their pale lives.

When my father told stories of how my red-haired, green-eyed grandmother slapped him down, a man six foot four, when he was thirty years old, how she threw butcher knives and irons when she was angry, he laughed about it with a kind of acceptance and even admiration. My grandmother had been brought up in an orphanage and raped when she was fifteen. Perhaps my father, a man prone to the same kinds of violent outbursts, felt that it was the life-force of her rage that had kept her alive, and perhaps he felt the ambivalence of one cowed by brutality in childhood, one who wants to be and admires the one who terrifies.

The last impression I want to give is that internalized racism is the fault of its victims. However, I feel deeply that we cannot think of racism as something "out there." It happens and is connected to the most profound and present shaping elements in our lives. The effects of the great social forces trickle down to the most vulnerable. Racism *is* a form of child abuse.

Ralph Ellison wrote about Richard Wright's ability to convert "the American Negro impulse toward self-annihilation and 'going-underground' into a will to confront the world, to evaluate his experience honestly and throw his findings unashamedly into the guilty conscience of America." It is not about memory, which can be an act of "recollect[ion] in tranquillity." It is a constant destruction of the self and the self's protection, an exploration of repression, an un-burying of what has been forgotten because memory could not tolerate the pain.

Twenty years to finish such a short book! Ten thousand revisions, several hundred thousand pages, exclusions, most destroyed, some put away. It's never right. Never does it say enough. Never does it say it in the right way. Never does it seem perfectly defensible as art, as truth, as solution, as anything. Never is it the right time. Never is it the right language. Never is it the right shape. Something is always incomplete, not said delicately enough, not with the right inflection. I haven't been "cured." I'm too light-skinned, too privileged for my suffering to have merit. I'm not a real "black" person. I'm too much of a victim. I don't offer hope. I say the same thing over. The problems I write about don't even exist anymore. Most of the time I left emotion out, I clung to facts—perhaps like a victim who distrusts her own story. I had to prove myself entitled to be believed. I had to prove myself an incontestable witness.

One of the things I've found out is that there are no simple answers. People do things at certain times in their lives, in their family's life, in history, for complex reasons, and we can't judge things in yes/no black/white terms. That's what it means to get beneath the surface of experience. We are all wounded by racism, but for some of us those wounds are anesthetized. None of us, black or white, wants to feel the pain that racism has caused. But when you feel it, you're awake.

T. S. Eliot spoke of "poetry so transparent that in reading it we are intent on what the poetry points at, and not on the poetry, this seems to me the thing to try for. To get beyond poetry, as Beethoven, in his last works, strove to get beyond music."

These things drive my writing: the insistence on clarity—not only clarity in form and language, but clarity in embodying our human nature, our "truth"— and on the integral connection between beauty, function, and drama. I want the eye of the reader, as in a house surrounded by beautiful and dramatic views, to be drawn away from the "house" itself, away from the writing, to what is around it.

This book is about the search for a home, a safe home for all our complexities, our beauty, and our abhorred life. It is about not finding that home in the world, and having to invent that home in language. Then aren't these square boxes on paper, not prose, but poems, houses for the heart to live in?

Once, teaching a class of young writers in a high school, I asked students to write about a first memory. One young man wrote a lucid account of his grandfather's face leaning over his crib when he was a baby. When I asked how he could remember something so early in his life, he said it was because his grandfather had died six months later. But I had always thought memory accrued in a chronological fashion. This memory had occurred because of something that had happened in the future. It made me realize that memory itself, rather than being absolute, linear, must be a continuous and liquid process, rather like the process that keeps the balance of crystals in a solution.

Coming to one's voice is also not a linear process, not a matter of learning skills, forms, and laws of grammar and syntax. It is a dynamic process in which much of what is occurring and has occurred remains invisible.

I am thinking of the many forces that come into play at every instant: psychological, cultural, social, spiritual, habitual processes that involve learning at its most intimate and personal level—how we respond to a loved one's approval and/or disapproval—as well as processes distant and completely out of our control—the availability of paper, pencils, books, the time to write. Since racism's most damaging insult is internal, to "self" as perception, it strikes me that, especially for a black writer, the process of coming to the creation of a great work of art is also a process that entails the re-creation and revision of the self.

W. E. B. Du Bois speaks of double consciousness. For me it isn't double, but many, many consciousnesses within. I say in one section of this book that I was watching the world as if I were looking through the eyes of the most vicious racist, but I was also looking through the eyes of white literary critics, black literary critics, of light-skinned black women and dark-skinned black women, of middle class and poor. I was looking through the eyes of my mother, cousins, and aunts. I had to find a way, not only to go around competing and repressive voices, but to address them, to listen and record, to disarm them and bring them to another perspective, to resolve conflicting aims. Voice becomes, not a synthesis of opposing voices, but rather a path of energy that is allowed by all sides, one that gains egress past restrictions by bowing to them at the same time they are disobeyed, by bargaining and earning. Each internal critic was the shaping edge I had to make my words vulnerable to, so that the voice of the inner critic became, not a voice to ignore, but a map to my own freedom, a marker for exactly where I had to go.

In the end, *The Black Notebooks* is about anything *but* "the truth." An entry I removed from the book says this:

When I read my notebooks over and read episodes that happened years ago that I have come to feel angry about, episodes in which I feel the other person said or did something that wounded me irreparably, I often find it recorded in a slightly different version than the one I had remembered. Frequently I find that the person I remember being so terrible to me had said or done something to ameliorate the hurt. In other words, what they did, as recorded immediately after the event, is not as bad as what they did years after in my memory. So that once again I doubt my ability to remember the "truth," "reality," and think that much of my memory must be resonant with a deep need to see myself as victim. I think that memory—they used to say that language is on the side of the country with the biggest navy—is in the service of the deepest psychic need.

We carry the unfinished business of the past forward. We are compelled to resolve, not only our personal wounds, but the wounds of our ancestors. It's as if we have been sent on their mission. We feel the painful wounds of history in our parents' bed.

Now I realize that the depression and fear of suicide that made me begin the work of this book was really a first re-memory of "killing" voices from my childhood. It was like feeling returning in a limb that has been asleep.

My need to keep a record, to remember what I had

forgotten in spite of the pain, to consciously bring about the same pain again, like making myself walk on a broken leg, was really the first movement toward health. I had to go back to those voices to find my way through and around them. The only difference was that this time I had words. It was language that saved my life.

This week, as I am readying the final manuscript for my editor, Jill Bialosky, I visit my mother, Antonia Baquet, and, during a conversation about writing, she reluctantly shares sections of the book that she has been writing for ten years, recollections of her life in the South and, especially, about her mother. I ask her if I can use excerpts from her book in my book so that another part of history can be added. She agrees. Combining our voices here, finding this harmony of purpose—in spite of the vast and excruciating separations between us (my primal "self" and "other")—is a revision of the creative act itself, not as an individual attainment but a dialogue of diverse voices, whose held complexities *are* resolution—perhaps even healing—are form.

Early Memory: The California Zephyr

What one does not remember dictates who one loves or fails to love. . . . What one does not remember is the serpent in the garden of one's dreams. What one does not remember is the key to one's performance in the toilet or in bed. What one does not remember contains the only hope, danger, trap, inexorability, of love—only love can help you recognize what you do not remember.

JAMES BALDWIN

I'm sure most people don't go around all the time thinking about what race they are. When you look like what you are, the external world mirrors back to you an identity consistent with your idea of yourself. However, for someone like me, who does not look like what I am, those mirrors are broken, and my consciousness or lack of consciousness takes on serious implications. Am I not conscious because, like others, I am just thinking of something else? Or is it because I don't want to be conscious? Am I mentally "passing"?

All my life I have passed invisibly into the white world, and all my life I have felt that sudden and alarming moment of consciousness when I remember I am black. It may feel like I'm emerging too quickly from deep in the ocean, or touching an electric fence, or like I'm a deer stuck in the headlights of an oncoming car. Sometimes in conversation with a white person who doesn't know I'm black, suddenly a feeling comes over me, a precursor—though nothing at all has been said about race—and I either wait helplessly for the other shoe to drop, try desperately to veer the conversation in another direction, or prepare myself for painful distinctions. My desire to escape is indistinguishable from my desire to escape from my "blackness," my race, and I am filled with shame and fury. I think the first time I became conscious of this internal state was when I was fifteen, on my way cross-country on a train, the California Zephyr.

The first day out, a young white man sat in the seat beside me. We had had a very pleasant conversation, but at night, when I grew tired, I asked him if he would go back to his seat so that I could stretch out. He said, "If you saw what's sitting in the seat beside me, you'd know why I can't go back." Of course, I knew without looking back what he meant, and as I stood up and turned around to see, I felt that now familiar combination of sickening emotions: hope that my sense of the situation was incorrect—in effect preferring to distrust my own perceptions—and fear that it wasn't, that my tender feelings for this man, and his feelings for me, were in mortal danger. If I spoke, I would make myself vulnerable. At the very least, he might categorize me in the same way he had categorized the other black person. If I didn't, I would be a coward, a betrayer of my people.

It seemed to me that even deeper than laws, than institutional practices, it was his invisible thoughts that hurt me. In fact, it seemed that, in a way, it is the combined thoughts, conscious and unconscious, of all of us that hold the machinery of racism in place, and in small remarks such as these, I am able to grasp, because I am allowed entry into it, a world of hatred so deep and hidden that it is impossible to address. This juncture in communication may seem so small an event in the history of racism, and of such indeterminate origins, that it is hardly worthy of speech. But it is precisely in such moments that I sense the local and engendering impulse, the twisted heart that keeps us locked in separate worlds of hate. It makes me despair of any real intimacy between blacks and whites.

I turned around and, sure enough, there was a young black man, a soldier, sitting in the seat. I said, very softly, "If you don't want to sit next to him, you don't want to sit next to me." I had hoped he'd be too stupid or deaf to understand. But he grew very quiet and said, after a few minutes, in an even softer voice than mine, "You're kidding." "No," I said. "You're kidding," he said again. "No," I said. "You're kidding." Each time he said it, he grew quieter. He excused himself. He may have slept in the bathroom. Every other seat was taken, and when I looked back to see if he was sleeping beside the soldier, the seat was empty.

The next morning, he found me on the way to breakfast and profusely apologized. "Please let me buy you breakfast," he said. I was lonely and wanted company, but I felt I had to punish him. I thought punishment was the only way he would gain respect for black people, and I felt the most effective kind of punishment was not verbal confrontation—which would probably only confirm his stereotypes of hostile blacks—but cool withdrawal. I had to punish myself, too, for I didn't want the pain of loneliness and alienation. I wanted and needed company, I liked him. But I felt in order to cut myself off from him, I had to cut off my feelings of tenderness and trust.

The last night on board, just before we were to arrive, I looked back and saw him sleeping beside the soldier. Perhaps he had gotten sick of sleeping in the bathroom, or perhaps my suffering had done some good.

The
Club

Herein lie buried many things which if read with patience may show the strange meaning of being black here in the dawning of the Twentieth Century. This meaning is not without interest to you, Gentle Reader; for the problem of the Twentieth Century is the problem of the color-line.

W. E. B. Du Bois

On Sunday afternoons Bruce and I would drive through the small bedroom communities close to New York, blocks and blocks of stately colonials and overpowering elms, and I would imagine a kind of life, a kind of happiness—a light on in an upstairs bedroom, a tricycle turned over in a drive, a swing on a front porch barely moving, as if it were just waiting for someone to come and sit down. I began to think that that was happiness. The happiness of expectancy. Everything that had to be prepared had been prepared, and now all that was needed was for the human heart to begin beating. I wanted to be in those houses, to be those people. I wanted to go all the way, as a pilot will make up his mind on a dangerous mission that there is no turning back. There were all kinds of practical reasons why we chose Upper Montclair, but, looking back, it was love that drove me through the streets of that unsuspecting city. Love.

September

Last month, seeing an advertisement in the newspaper for a contemporary in our price range, I called an agent. "I shouldn't be telling you about this on the phone," she said, "but there is a house I think you would be interested in. It's on an estate on Highland Avenue, and the people are very particular about who buys it."

My heart shriveled. Should I find out whom they are "particular" not to have? Should I let her think I'm white and go without Bruce to see it? When I take Bruce, we are shown entirely different neighborhoods, all-black or integrated.

I decided to act dumb. "Oh, really? That seems strange. Why isn't the house multiple-listed? What are they so careful about?"

"Well, you know, some people like to do it this way. Let me have your phone number; I'll call you back." But she never called back. So I wonder if our name is known—"That black couple looking for a house in town and the wife looks white."

This week I called another agent and played a game. "We'd like to look at the house you're describing, but we'd also like to see a house we heard about on an estate."

"Oh," she gargled, "you mean, ah, the one that came on the market this morning?"

"I don't know when it came on the market, but I *do* know it's on Highland Ave."

"I don't know if you'd be interested in that. The rooms are small, it's overgrown, overpriced, no view." She went on and on. I was still interested.

"Well," she finally agreed, "I'll see if I can get the owners on the phone and we can go and see it."

When Bruce and I got to her office, of course she hadn't gotten hold of them. "The man works at night. No one is at home."

"I'd still like to see it. Drive by on the way to the other house." She got lost! Imagine a real estate dealer getting lost in her own town!

"That's all right," I reassured her. "We can go past it on the way back."

The house she showed us, in the integrated part of town, was expensive and run-down. On the way to the "particular" house, once again she got lost. We had to direct her. Bruce said, "There it is! There it is!" It was all lit up. And she kept driving. Finally, a half mile down the road (I was waiting to see if she would ever stop), I said, "Why didn't you stop at the house?"

"Oh," she stammered, "did we pass it?"

"My husband pointed it out to you."

"It's so dark, I can't find it. It's too dark tonight. I think we should come back tomorrow."

"I don't mind the dark."

"You mean you want me to turn around and go *back?*" she gasped.

When we got to the house, we sat in the car while she "checked." We could see in the front window. Two old ladies were reading the paper. She came back and said they didn't want visitors.

I felt a hopelessness descend. No matter how clever and determined I am, they can always find a way to stop me. Perhaps I should call a lawyer, sue. . . . But it would probably take forever, and I'd need a courage and commitment that I don't feel. I decide to look for a house in another community, one where we are not yet known, and this time I'll go to the real estate agent's alone.

October

It's the overriding reality I must get through. Each time I drive down the streets and see only whites, each time I notice no blacks in the local supermarket or walking on the streets, I think, *I'm not supposed to be here.* When I go into real estate agents' offices, I put on a mask. At first they hope you are in for a quick sell. They show you houses they want to get rid of. But if you stick around, and if you are the "right kind," they show you ones just newly listed, and sometimes not even on the market. There are neighborhoods that even most white people are not supposed to be in.

I make myself likable, optimistic. I am married, a woman who belongs to a man. Sometimes I reveal I am Catholic, if it might add a feeling of connection. It is not entirely that I am acting. I am myself but slightly strained, like you might strain slightly in order to hear something whispered.

Yesterday an agent took me into the most lily-white neighborhood imaginable, took me right into the spotless kitchen, the dishwasher rumbling, full of the children's dishes. I opened the closets as if I were a thief, as if I were filthying them, as if I believe about myself what they believe: that I'm "passing," that my silence is a crime.

The first woman I knew about who "passed" was the bronze-haired daughter of insurance money, one of the wealthiest black families in the United States. I remember my mother telling me stories of her white roadster, how she wrote plays and opened a theater. She had directed several of the plays in which my mother and father had acted. She went to New York to "make it" and was published in *The New York Times*. I was seven when my father went down to meet the midnight train that brought her home: people said she had confessed to her rich fiancé that she was black and he had jilted her. They dressed her in a long bronze dress, a darkened tone of her long auburn hair. She looked like Sleeping Beauty in a casket made especially for her with a glass top.

My mother told me how, when she was young, her

mother used to get great pleasure when she would seat her daughter in the white part of the train and then depart, as if she were her servant. She said her mother would stand alongside the train and wave good-bye with a smile on her face, like a kid who has gotten away with the cookies. And my father told how, during the Detroit riots of 1943, when black men were being pulled off the buses and beaten to death, he used to walk down East Grand Boulevard as a dare.

Of course, we are never caught; it is absolutely inconceivable that we could go unrecognized, that we are that much like them. In fact, we are the same.

When Bruce and I first got married, I had been looking for an apartment for months. Finally, I found a building in a nice neighborhood with a playground nearby, and a school that was integrated. I rang the bell and was relieved when the supervisor who came to the door was black. I loved the apartment. Then I became terrified. Should I tell *him* we're black? Would that make my chances of getting the apartment greater? I wondered if he would be glad to have another black family in the building, or if maybe his job was dependent on his keeping us out. I decided to be silent, to take the chance that he liked me.

When I left, sailing over the George Washington Bridge, I had my first panic attack. I thought I might drive my car right over the edge. I felt so high up there, so disconnected, so completely at my own mercy. Some part of me doesn't give a fuck about boundaries—in fact, sees the boundaries and is determined to dance over them no matter what the consequences are. I am so precarious, strung out between two precipices, that even when I get to the other side, I am still not down, still not so low I can't harm myself.

I could hardly control my car, my heart pounding, my hands sweaty on the wheel. I had to pull off the West Side Highway as soon as I could, and I went into the first place I could find, a meat-packing house. The kind white man let me use the phone to call Bruce before he took me in a big meat truck to the nearest hospital. The doctor said it was anxiety, and I should just go home and rest. For days I was afraid to come out of my house, and even now, though I push myself to do it, every time I go over a high place, or am in a strange territory, I fear I will lose control, that something horrible and destructive will come out of me.

Each night Bruce and I don't talk about it, as if there were no cost to what I'm doing, or as if whatever the cost is I've got to pay.

March

I had told the real estate dealers that Bruce was away on a long trip—I had looked at over eighty houses!—and that I had to make the decision by myself. At night, under cover of darkness, we'd go back and circle the houses and I'd describe the insides.

In Maplewood, a nearby town in which I had looked, the real estate agent took us to the house I had seen alone the day before—a dark, sturdy Tudor—without seeming to bat an eye. However, when we got back to his office and were ready to close the deal, the head broker had intervened. "That house has been sold," he said.

Our agent looked shocked. "No it hasn't," he said stupidly. "I just checked the listing before we went out!"

"Yes it has," the other insisted.

We had called a lawyer who specializes in civil

rights cases and he had not been encouraging. "These kinds of cases are hard to prove and your money will be tied up for months."

We finally decided on Upper Montclair. The houses in Essex County are comparatively cheaper than the houses in Bergen County, and even though the neighborhoods aren't integrated, the schools are, since busing is in effect. Many afternoons, instead of asking—not wanting to arouse the suspicions of the real estate agents—I would sit outside the neighborhood schools at lunch hour like a pederast, counting the number of black faces. Though sometimes I'd be brave and ask. I didn't only want information; I wanted to commit a small revolutionary act—to leave the impression that the world is full of liberal white parents who want change.

When Bruce finally saw the house in Upper Montclair, he said, "It's all right. I liked the Tudor much better." I was furious. Didn't he know how hard I had tried! "Next time *you* look at eighty houses," I had burst out on the way home. At each point, even as we accomplished our goals, we didn't feel proud of ourselves and confirmed in our powers, we felt divided, muted, and out of control.

The real estate dealer in Montclair had been flustered when Bruce showed up at her office. I had hoped that, maybe, since I had purposely let slip he is a vice president at the bank and has hundreds of people working for him (Bruce has the highest position of any black person at the bank), she would decide, as many whites have, that a person with his credentials, whose skin and hair is, in the least, indeterminate, must be something else, Spanish or Arab. But when we signed the contract, she had insisted she and her husband pick up the deposit at our apartment, though it was a half-hour drive. They want to check us out, I thought. I cleaned all day, fixed hors d'oeuvres. I opened a bottle of champagne and we toasted each other, as if we were friends.

During the months we waited for the closing, neither one of us went to the house. We didn't want to rock the boat. Several times minor problems arose, and I couldn't decide whether to get very involved, to bother people, or to stay out of the way.

The week before we moved in, I made a dozen trips with lamps, paintings, books. Emptied of the lady's furniture, the walls showed hand prints, rubs; the carpet was drab, muddied, there was a dinginess to the light. Had they gotten rid of a loser? A few days after, Bruce warned: "Be careful, they know more about us than you think!" A neighbor had come up to him while he was out shoveling snow. "I hear you're a V.P. at the bank and a Michigan man!" Bruce hadn't told *anybody* where he worked or went to school!

Last week the people across the street gave us a cocktail party. I felt grateful, but out of place. Would I break a glass or say something unforgivable? I couldn't get over the feeling that I had to prove myself different from what I was sure almost all of them took for granted—that Bruce and I didn't know anything about wine or art and had never seen an Oriental carpet in our lives—yet at the same time, I had to be absolutely "myself," *that* was the only way I could earn their respect. I told one woman she had the most beautiful violet eyes—I found out later she was the wife of the president of one of the largest New York brokerage houses—and she looked shocked. She avoided me the rest of the night. Was it wrong to confess love as well as hatred? Suddenly, right in the middle of my urgent desire to belong, came my hatred of them and everything they stood for.

Bruce and I went our separate ways, like those black people who have learned not to sit together in the lunchroom. Sometimes I looked at him from across the room and thought, he looks so uncomfortable. It comes out in the way he spills his drink or drops some dip on his tie and then calls attention to himself: "I spilled something," he says, looking down and dabbing it with his handkerchief.

I know that way we stumble, trying so hard, how something gets blocked so that we either become hard and inflexible or so muted we can't be heard, or maybe something gets out of control, so that no matter what we do, for how long, for countless years, finally we make some mistake, something that we can't make up for, and we don't know why, can't stop ourselves, and, in the end, we are more sorry for our mistake than the ones it hurt.

April

Montclair is divided into two parts, Upper and—though not referred to as such on maps—so-called Lower. A neighbor said that a hundred years ago Upper Montclair was where the rich people lived and Lower Montclair was where the people lived who worked for them. There are lots of mansions and estates on that side of town, but even so, in a way, an invisible map has grown into the nerves and bones of the people, a reference not only to geography but to the importance of the self, who you are in relation to the other. The map is pressed into the feet of the children. The dividing line is Watchung Avenue—you're on one side or the other.

The kids are mixed in the schools because of busing, but lots of white families, and some black, still try to stop it. Just because the kids are in school together doesn't mean things are better. Things seem to be worse. There is a great deal of pain when the dividing line is broken. It is like breaking the self in two. We have nothing to heal it, and no medicine to relieve the pain. We think, Break it and it will heal itself. We just don't know whether it will grow together in such a crooked way that it will never be able to be used.

We know so little—almost nothing about how the cells become part of the body—whether to root the sickness out with surgery, whether that will destroy too many healthy parts, or whether to take tiny pills, every day, for the rest of our lives, to admit we have a chronic disease that we must attend to.

I ran into a woman at the vet's today, a white woman married to a black man whose son is very, very dark. We got into a heavy conversation about Montclair, and when I told her I was black, she couldn't believe it. She wanted to know what color my parents were. I think she feels sad that her son is so dark. She said she and her husband had had a daughter, but they "lost" her (a miscarriage?). She never saw her. I guess, looking at me, she wondered what color her daughter would have been.

This woman wanted her son to have the best education, so she put him in a private school in Montclair. But there was so much prejudice, she took him out. He's now in one of the lowest sections in public school. She says he's very bright, but he told her he liked being the smartest kid in the group. He told her, "Don't worry, Mom. I don't want to ever be anything really big. I just want to get by." He's in the sixth grade.

She told me they couldn't get an apartment in Upper Montclair because of her son. When they saw her, fine, but when they saw her son, no way. She said finally they bought a house and as soon as they moved in the neighbors called the law. They had to spend ten thousand dollars on repairs right away. She said she's not running. She's not going no place. If anyone runs, it will be them. She says she doesn't make friends with anyone. Since she's married a black man, she's realized the only real friends you have are your family. She says she's happy with her life. It's the other people who must be unhappy to do all these things. She's just fine.

July

This morning I put my car in the shop. The neighborhood shop. When I went to pick it up I had a conversation with the man who had worked on it. I told him I had been afraid to leave the car there at night with the keys in it. "Don't worry," he said. "You don't have to worry about stealing as long as the niggers don't move in." I couldn't believe it. I hoped I had heard him wrong. "What did you say?" I asked. He repeated the same thing without hesitation.

In the past, my anger would have swelled quickly. I would have blurted out something, hotly demanded he take my car down off the rack immediately, though he had not finished working on it, and taken off in a blaze. I love that reaction. The only feeling of power one can possibly have in a situation in which there is such a sudden feeling of powerlessness is to "do" something, handle the situation. When you "do" something, everything is clear. But this is the only repair shop in the city. Might I have to come back here someday in an emergency?

Blowing off steam is supposed to make you feel better. But in this situation it *doesn't!* After responding in anger, I often feel sad, guilty, frightened, and confused. Perhaps my anger isn't just about race. Perhaps it's like those rapid-fire responses to Bruce—a way of dulling the edge of feelings that lie even deeper.

I let the tension stay in my body. I go home and sit with myself for an hour, trying to grasp the feeling—the odor of self-hatred, the biting stench of shame.

July

Last week a young woman who lives down the street came over for dinner. She's thirty, the daughter of a doctor. She lived in New York for a few years on her own, lost her job, may have had a breakdown, and came home to "get herself together."

After dinner we got into a conversation about Tall Oaks Country Club, where she is the swimming instructor. I asked her, hesitantly, but unwilling not to get this information, if blacks were allowed to join. (Everybody on our block belongs; all were told about "the club" and asked to join as soon as they moved in. We were never told or asked to join.)

"No," she said.

"You mean the people on this block who have had us over for dinner, who I have invited to my home for dinner, I can't swim in a pool with them?"

"That's the rule," she said, as if she were stating a mathematical fact. She told us about one girl, the daughter of the president of a bank, who worked on the desk at Tall Oaks. When they told her blacks couldn't join, she quit. I wondered why she told this—the swimming instructor—as if she wasn't ashamed of herself.

I remembered how once she had looked at pictures in our family album and seen my mother's house.

"This is like one of the houses on Upper Mountain Avenue," she had exclaimed. "I didn't know black people had homes like this!"

I have begun therapy—with a white therapist—and when I told him about how disturbed I was by this conversation, he said he didn't believe that people were like this anymore. He said I would have to try to join to be able to tell. He told me it had something to do with how I see myself as deprived by my family, my neurosis.

Four days ago Ann called, the woman down the street, asking if my son could baby-sit. I like this woman. I don't know why. She has that red hair and ruddy coloring out of a Rubens painting. Easy to talk to. She and her husband are members of the club, and I couldn't resist telling her the story.

She said, "Oh, Toi, John and I wanted to invite you and Bruce to be our guests at a dinner party. I was just picking up the phone to call when Holly [a woman who lives across the street] called and said, 'Do you think that's a good idea? You better check with the Stevens [old members of the club] first.' I called George and he called a meeting of the executive committee. We met for four hours. Several of us said we would turn in our resignations unless you could come. But the majority felt it wouldn't be a good idea because you would see all the good things and want to join, and since you couldn't join, it would just hurt you and be frustrating. John and I wanted to quit. I feel very ashamed of myself, but the next summer, when I was stuck in the house with the kids and nothing to do, we started going again."

When I related this to my therapist, he said it sounded like my feelings about my mother. I see my mother as having something that she is keeping from me, some love that I can't get from her. He said that all this feeling of deprivation is really because I can't get to the sadness of living without her.

Yesterday the executive board of Poets & Writers of New Jersey met to read the poetry of a new applicant. I am a member. Right away I said to myself, "The poetry is too loose. Not precise enough. She's not ready." But soon after I recognized certain colloquialisms, settings. *She is probably black,* I thought.

I know these people are very particular about who they let in. They vote no on just about everybody. I'm usually the one who believes that seriousness is the best criterion for entrance. I got terrified. Would I have to stand up for this woman's work against all these people? How could I do so when I didn't really believe in it? Was I judging her too harshly because she is black? Was I putting myself down by judging her harshly? Could I hear her voice inside these poems? Or am I too brainwashed by the sound of Yeats, Eliot, Lowell, Plath? What was I expecting? I went foggy. If I was going to have to fight for her, I'd do it. But I prayed I wouldn't have to. She had to get in. Her voice had to have a place.

Luckily, everyone in the group said she was good. I put her poems back on the table. I didn't say anything.

August

It's the loneliness I can't take, the way the house stuffs up with it like a head that can't breathe. The sun coming through the glass in the middle of the afternoon magnifies perfection. Everything's right: The floors shine with an underlife like the several colors in a woman's hair, the chandelier's sounding brilliance, the little islands of furniture placed like this and this, the red throw's splash of color. Everything wakes me as if my feet were electrified. My eyes are driven outward, out of my body. Such cleanliness hates me; it wants me to concede to its beauty. It asks, *Are you doing your part? Did you turn the burner off? Did you check the gas? Did you take the keys?* "Did you" has a life of its own, a furious life that could commit murder and put the blame on me! Oh boiler in the basement, red eye of some miserable housewife, or some child locked in the basement with spiders. Yesterday, taking the clothes down into the dark, I felt that emptiness at the top of a scream. I feel the atmosphere, like a woman in a huge tank walking underwater. The house is so large it never ends. Or else I am lying on my back like an upturned turtle. Am I dreaming they hate me? Am I dreaming the house, the block, the neighborhood? Is the whole world my evil dream?

My son comes home. I make all the right motions. I move the pots, my lips ask questions. I reassure. I'm not pretending! I can become the actual thing. It animates me, like a machine that knows its own duties. It's hardest when Bruce comes home, when part of me for an instant hopes, when I can almost touch the end of loneliness—like a smell you can almost name.

Each night we sit in the TV dark. He is calm, contained. Sometimes I tell him I don't feel love. One time I even went back to Detroit, to my mother's house. But he came and got me and just said, "Get in the car." Such love I don't deserve! The best thing I can do is keep my mouth shut. But he opens the door, puts his coat away, and speaks, and his actual weight enters me. When I come home late, I notice our bedroom windows mildly lit, just like the windows of the house next door.

It makes you have to bear it, like a cross, like the

weight of a body that isn't there, like a blessing you go on and on expecting, until it burns you raw, sharpens, and turns to pain.

August

I haven't slept much at all for several weeks, and when I do I dream of shit, overflowing toilets, water and shit up to my ankles. A few weeks ago I was at the doctor's office and picked up an issue of *Time*. I see that a comet is coming toward the earth and a feeling came over me as if I were paralyzed, in a box without a key. I keep seeing the comet, like that dream I had when I was twelve when my mother and father were divorcing, the moon and sun rushing toward each other. I sit up in bed all night, or fall asleep and dream dreams I can't bear to remember.

My father called last night to say he was sending my half-brother this summer and I wanted to scream, "How dare you assume I'll take care of your son, your precious son, when you didn't do a goddamned thing for me!" But I didn't. I said OK so fast it was as if I didn't even need to think it over. I love my brother and am happy to see him. But I am depressed and I can hardly take care of myself and my own family.

I am reading a book by Arthur Janov called *The Primal Scream*. I heard John Lennon used this form of therapy. There was a pain locked up inside him since childhood about his mother abandoning him, and the only way he could express it was by letting himself go, screaming until the deepest part of his pain came to the surface. I'm terrified to do this, that I might start screaming and never stop, but I'm desperate to get better, so tonight I creep downstairs to the basement when everyone is sleeping. It is two o'clock and I am so frightened of the darkness, the furnace's glowing eye, the thousand leggers and spiders, my whole body is cold. I go down on all fours like an animal, I put a pillow over my mouth so that I won't wake anybody, and I start to scream. At first it is a small scream, as if I know what I am doing, but the longer I scream, the more crazy I sound. I scream and I can't remember what the scream before sounded like. I hear myself call my grandmother's name, the one whose breast I sucked until I was seven and she died. The one who wasn't afraid of my father. "Re," I scream, "Re." I want her to come back and protect me.

Bruce comes down in his tee shirt and jockey shorts. There must be a moon out because I see his naked thighs and forearms lit up in a slash of silvery light as he comes down the stairs, slowly, as if he's sinking in water. He seems afraid to touch me. He speaks softly, "Are you all right?" I tell him to go back to bed. What can he do? He has to go to work tomorrow. He can't stay up all night and hold me. And he won't. Even when he tries, he falls asleep. I feel his body trying, it jerks a little, and then he falls off to that slow regular breathing, and I know I am alone.

I go back upstairs and sit at the dining room table in the dark. I sit there under the chandelier I've cleaned until the dark sets it to music. It makes a clear inhuman sound, as if it has no memory of touch.

I pick up a pencil and open my notebook. I can't think of anything to write, just little marks like chicken scratch. The only words that come are: "Like a tree in hostile soil."

February

Last night we had two couples over for dinner: the Alvarezes, the first friends Bruce made when he moved to New York; and the Kings, new friends who live in this area. Charles King is the first black vice principal of one of the neighboring city's junior high schools, a position that, in many cases, has been reserved for a black man, somebody who can discipline black students without being accused of racism.

Before long we got to talking about Tall Oaks. Charles and his wife related experiences they had had. Charles had tried to buy a home in Upper Montclair about ten years ago. The night he looked at it someone burned a cross on the lawn. It shouldn't surprise me, but it *does* surprise me that in 1968 people were still burning crosses—not down South, but way, way up North. He remembers that when he was a boy, a black kid couldn't walk down the street in the neighboring town, Glen Ridge. It was a big joke to the kids. They knew they could always save the dime carfare by walking over to Glen Ridge Avenue; the cops would pick them up and drive them to the border of Montclair.

Ray Alvarez thinks we have a good lawsuit. They can't keep us out of the club because we're black; it's illegal. He was turned on to finding a good lawyer. Bruce was hesitant. He said, "White money sticks together. They'll get back at us where it hurts—in the pocketbook." I'm sure he was thinking about his job at the bank.

After dinner I noticed that the dining room window was open. I thought back on the heated discussion we had had. How passionate we had been—angry, loud. If someone had been out walking a dog or coming home late, they would have heard us. I felt like glass. Now they would know the anger that was under that polite woman who held conversations with them over their fences about wallpaper, an enraged black woman who called them "fucking assholes!"

In bed that night, I felt unsure of my anger. Had I just been saying those things about my neighbors to fit in with the others? Is it the story of my life to try to get along with whomever I am with—not knowing who I really love, to which group belongs my true allegiance?

I remembered an incident from childhood. When I was about nine, I was passionately in love with my cousin. I thought she didn't love me as much as I loved her. One day she was very angry at our aunt and started saying things about her—the way we often talked about adults when we were angry. I didn't believe these things. My aunt had been kind to me all my life. But I felt that in order to win my cousin's love, I had to accede to the things she said—and I made up a few of my own. Suddenly my aunt opened the door. She had heard everything. My relationship with her was never the same.

I lie in bed wondering who and what I love. Who I identify with. Who I am. Suddenly a terrible fear comes over me, so real it is in my throat, in my mouth, so great it could swallow me. My neighbors had heard. They knew what I really was like and now they hated me. They would hurt me and my family. They would kill us. It was so real—the way fears can be when the defenses of the day are stripped away.

If we sued, I would be terrified. I wouldn't be able to sleep or eat. How had those people in the South during the civil rights struggle stood up? I would go mad or commit suicide—as if what they think of me were more powerful than what I think of myself. As if I could be eaten up by another's idea.

This week the first edition of *Who's Who in Black America* came out. Bruce's name is in it. Married to Toinette Webster. One son, Anthony.

Who's who

in black

America?

February

Bruce has agreed to see a marriage counselor. He doesn't want to, but he knows things are not going well between us. Some days I feel this great rush of anticipation before he comes home. I feel lightened and happy. But when he opens the door and I see his face, it is as if the person I was waiting for disappears.

Last Saturday I made him go out for groceries with me. We had to wait in line for gas for a half hour. All the time I was telling him my writing was just as important as his work, even though I don't have a full-time job. He can't expect me to do all the house-work, the grocery shopping, the cleaning. When we got home, he went to the dining room to do taxes and I was screaming that I wanted him to help me put the groceries away.

Suddenly I heard a terrible sound from the dining room, like an animal gored in the heart. When I came into the room, he was screaming with his eyes forced shut and his teeth clenched. His feet were up in the air and he was shaking all over. "I just can't take it," he said. "I just can't!" I stood back in horror. I've only seen Bruce angry twice in ten years and never any-thing like this. I didn't know what to do. Finally he bent over the table and wept. I led him upstairs to the bathroom to wipe his face as if he were a patient in a hospital. When I looked at his eyes, pus was coming out—pus! As if a huge infected wound had broken open inside him. Our son came in and we sat around him terrified and trying to comfort him. "I'm all right," he said finally, his voice flat. *What have I done?* I thought. And I didn't know whether it would help if I moved closer, or moved away.

August

Why should I think that when people see Bruce and me together they assume I'm black? Friends have said to me, "Why would they think you're black just because you're with Bruce? They would still assume you're white, just think you're a white woman married to a black man." When I'm with Bruce, I *feel* black, feel as if I'm taken in by his blackness, as if his blackness falls on me, as if it casts a powerful shadow. Perhaps I assume we become the things we love, and I assume everyone else can see. And there is another reason. There is a part of me that would rather be perceived as a black woman who is a black man's wife than to be perceived as a white woman who is a black man's wife.

When I was growing up, among the black middle and upper classes, it was thought to be "marrying down" for a black man to marry a white woman. In a world in which we had been so punished by exclusion, we made rules by which *we* could exclude. We created local and national clubs. People gained entrance based on their color, money, education, job, how long their family had been rooted, successful, and visible. We created a society in which we too had people we were better than, people we could aspire to be. We really believed we were better. Those of us who, given all the circumstances, had not only sur-

vived but survived with distinction, had something
we didn't want tainted. When I was growing up, I was
never intimidated by white people. Black people were
the masters of intimidation.

I remember many young men telling the story of
how, on the first date, they got the third degree in the
foyer of the old Brown mansion. Mrs. Brown would
come down before Beverly, ask the boy to take a seat
on the settee, and ask about his family. Though most
families weren't as obvious, the thought was the
same. Stick to your own kind. The very exclusion that
our society had perpetrated on us had, as far as we
were concerned, created a special blood, a psychological advantage.

Sometimes, amazingly, blacks and whites are allied
in their hatreds. I had heard talk about white women
who had married black soldiers, willing, as they said,
to do *anything* to get to this country. I had heard talk
about some poor white trash caught in the net of her
father's hatred, who had fallen on a black man's penis
and worshiped it like God. In the eyes of both blacks
and whites, those women were hated. A touch of love
across the races is abhorred. And perhaps that is the
suspicion that lingers about one such as me.

When I'm with Bruce, it is as if I'm taken under
the wing of his blackness, as if I become him, or of
him, like Eve taken from the body of Adam. Whatever
is tainted of him is also tainted of me; whatever is
beloved of him is also beloved of me. I become what
he is in restaurants, in real estate offices, at times
reluctantly, but without question.

Do I, given my place of trembling identity, slip over
and become the thing I am closest to? If so, no wonder I married a black man! To have married a white
man would have been terrifying, to love a white man

would have made me feel constantly adrift from the most primitive cells. How frightening to be awash without constructs! To be placed outside the walls of the city! To lose kinship, memory, and begin again with nothing, a liquid self, as I do again and again each day.

Sometimes when I lie down beside him I feel like a little girl lying on her mother's breast. In my dreams he is shining like Christ, so beautiful. What is this love that takes me in, that reflects back my own goodness? "You are so good," he whispers when we make love.

Knowing whom we love and hate holds reality in place. His body protects me, stands between me and a kind of annihilation.

April

I see them going out together on Friday nights. I peek through the shutters when I hear their voices in the street. It's as if they're showing off, the way some people will get you by laughing loudly and seeming to have a good time. They come out, all at the same time: the Baldwins walk across the street and get into the Lloyds' car, the Stevens wave at them as they pull out of their drive. They're all going to the club for dinner or a party. The ladies have on long skirts, Ann a kind of satin plaid—always so unselfconscious, so thrown together and yet so right, and poor Holly has tried so hard and is looking so uncomfortable in her clothes.

Sometimes they're laughing, making little jokes I can't quite understand, tinkling their keys. The Merrills and Grahams come out together. They've had a little before-dinner drink—straight shots of bourbon for the men and a mixed drink with a cherry for the ladies—though they like their drinks strong, maybe a Manhattan. They parade in front of me as if I weren't at home, as if I wouldn't notice and feel left out. What have I done wrong? Why can't I please them? I'm much more fun, more interesting than that pale Holly Baldwin and her boring husband, and yet they take them along. And they make noise out there, the noise of happiness, as if they want me to hear it and be sad.

I used to watch my mother when she bathed, I'd peek through the keyhole of the bathroom. It aroused me, the way she lay there unsuspecting. It wasn't that I thought she was beautiful, though she was beautiful, in every sense of that word, but that I was so over-powered by what I saw that I didn't know the lan-guage for it. Her breasts were large, with just a little droop, and paler than the rest of her. I had seen the fine spider veins in them those times my father rubbed her with Ben-Gay, and sometimes she'd ask me to do it, to make her rheumatism better. When she'd emerge, I'd see the pubic hair glistening. I'd often see it when she'd take off her girdle after work and sit on the floor in her slip with her legs open, cut-ting and painting her toenails. I felt I had to take what I wanted, steal it, that it was impossible to have my need satisfied in any other way. I had to steal glances, and in some way, I felt she wanted me to, as if there was no other way for her to teach me what it is to be a woman.

So many silences in our house, so much we did that no one spoke about or volunteered to explain, as if we never depended on language. We seemed trapped in a languageless world in which it was necessary to hap-pen on the other at a moment of vulnerability, that it was impossible to know each other in any other way.

April

I haven't written here for a couple of days now. It takes tremendous discipline to push myself to the typewriter. I keep thinking, *Not much has happened today.* Yet, when I sit down and think, I realize that many things have happened that are related to my feelings about being black. It always surprises me that this is true. Like dreams, these experiences slip easily into unconsciousness. Perhaps like the thought of one's own death, one can't do much except forget.

Now I understand why so many older black people are hesitant to talk about their childhoods. I tried to get my great-uncle to tell me about his childhood— what the town was like, what his family life was like, what his mother was like. (I didn't bother to ask him about his father because I sensed, having heard that my great-grandmother had six children, by three different men, that might be an embarrassing question.) He kept telling me he didn't like thinking about the old days. He said he'd stopped doing that long ago. "The past is over and done with," and he kept shaking his head.

Why not talk about the past? He had certainly survived, and that was the most important thing. I felt that if he didn't talk, some part of us, our history, would die, and it seemed he was giving consent, as if he was saying death is better.

I oppose that forgetfulness. We have so few clues to lead us. We must remember as much as we can. I pressed and he told two stories.

His first remembrance had to do with the land his mother owned, a small piece of property and a house that had been passed down for three generations. It had originally been given, under an unwritten agreement, by the wealthy plantation owner for whom our family worked and whose land their house bordered. Other "privileged" Negroes lived there, "uptown," in small houses, too. When my uncle was two years old, a sheriff came and told his mother—and her six children—they had to be out in forty-eight hours. When she told him that the land had been given to her mother, he said, "Show me the deed." Of course, there wasn't any, proving that all black people have is what white people aren't using at the time.

A man had paid one dollar for the title to each lot that the black people lived on, and my great-grandmother's family, as well as more than a hundred of their neighbors, were dispossessed. The following year, the man founded one of the first hot-sauce companies and paid the people who had lived on the land ten cents a bushel—the job took the better part of a day—to pick red peppers. My uncle said that he and his sons were millionaires before my uncle was a grown man.

He told another story: When Uncle Lawrence was twelve, he had a minor disagreement with one of the young white boys who lived in the town. The boy hit him and he returned the blow. The boy and his friend took off after Uncle, who was making off as fast as he could down the main street. As he ran through the business section, he must have attracted the attention of the proprietors of stores and their customers because, when Uncle reached the office of the dentist for whom he worked and turned around, there were close to fifty people behind him. Uncle ran into the office of the dentist, a man he had been working for for years, and seeing that Uncle was in trouble, the dentist pulled a new revolver from his drawer—a gun that had only recently been invented—and met the crowd on the stairs. "What's the matter?"

"That nigger hit a white boy."

"Boy, come over here. Did you hit a white boy?"

"Yes, sir, but I wouldn't hit him if he hadn't hit me first."

"See here. This nigger has worked for me for years and he wouldn't hit nobody that didn't hit him first. Now all you folks get the hell out of here before I blow your brains out."

As soon as they left, the dentist pulled him aside. "Nigger, don't you ever let me hear of you hitting a white boy again," and he pointed the revolver at Uncle's head, "or I'll kill you myself."

Uncle left home as soon as he could—soon after that—and never went back to see his mother, Philomean Durante, again. She was mean to her children, he said, never spoke to them, and sometimes, when she was boiling white people's clothes in a big iron pot in their yard, she'd fish out a steaming, wet towel and strike at the legs of the children as they ran by. But the thing he could never forgive her for was how she fed the poor children in the neighborhood, anyone who came, though many nights her own children went to bed hungry. "Share what you got," he remembers her saying.

Sometimes memory is like a dream. The worst nightmares are forgotten. Sometimes living is a nightmare. Just getting up, meeting your neighbors, and walking down the street.

Today I was in the supermarket and saw two of my neighbors. I cannot bring myself to say anything about what's happened. I know it sounds crazy, but I don't want to put them on the spot. These two: the young woman down the street who lives with her parents, who struggles with the question of whether or not to get braces on her teeth, who I hear had a breakdown and can't get a job. What would I say to her? And why? And the other neighbor, a woman who almost died during her last two pregnancies, is trying again.

Why aren't their gestures enough? I know they can't go any further. Even the conversations that take place day after day in which no one hurts me, the ride to the grocery store, the laughter and the exchange of recipes and decorators' names over the backyard fence, it isn't enough. Yet I know they have given all they can. And more than others. The next day when I see them, it is common loneliness that makes me speak.

May

A boy was shot by a policeman and the black community is very upset. He had taken his father's car, a police car, and he and several other boys had driven to a neighboring town, had a few drinks, and were returning. Stopped by the police, they scattered in all directions. The boy who was shot allegedly approached the policeman with a tire iron. The cop killed him.

A spokesman for the black community said this boy was not the kind of kid foolish enough to approach a policeman holding a gun with a tire iron. He said he was not accusing the policeman of being a racist, but saying that this probably would not have happened if the boy had been white.

I remembered the afternoon I was driving down Erie Street, turned a corner, and saw ten or fifteen black boys standing in the middle of the street. My heart beat faster, my breathing quickened. I thought they might pull open my door and attack me. As my logical mind began to work, my fear decreased. There were girls mixed in the group. They were playing a game, maybe catch. My breathing went back to normal. But I was ashamed. Would my reaction have been the same if I had seen ten white boys? The fight-or-flight response, adrenaline to the muscles and heart, is connected to the deepest and most automatic parts of the brain. In certain circumstances, survival may depend on reactions that occur instantly, without thought. But how had these boys—just because they were black—tripped that wire in me that made them a blur of danger? Was my reaction any different from the white policeman's? Would I have pulled the trigger?

December

Reluctantly, reluctantly, I become what he is in restaurants, in hotels, reluctantly. I try to beat him to the counter so that the woman won't give us a room in which they put the niggers. Reluctantly I become what he is, again and again, reluctantly.

> Niggers and flies,
> I do despise,
> but the more I see niggers,
> the more I like flies.

You might think I learned that from a white man, but I didn't. I learned it from a black man, one of my uncles, who sang it to me, laughing it up close to my face, a taunt, a joke on somebody he thought wasn't him. Wasn't it about him? About us? Or were we held apart, separated by some invisible skin, not exactly color—because so many who sang that song were dark—but by some kind of thinking that certainly white people couldn't see. If we just kept singing it, then it would happen, like cream separates from milk, we children in a circle, clapping our hands, dancing the funniness of it into our bones, knitting it to the marrow, so that we might have to be killed to draw it out, split in two, eviscerated. My uncle coming up close with his "nigger" face, a horrible mirror. I see a black man walking down the street and I recoil: *It is <u>he</u> that is more despicable, not I.*

> (He is a blur of color,
>   a slight hue,
>
>   a pigment that falls
>   like a shadow
>   on the eye. *I*
> am something different.)

Didn't my ancestors pray for something like me, wanting a way out of their nightmares? My uncle warning, "Don't bring any of those dark boys home!"

My mother's mother took breakfast to her daughter on a silver tray, figs and cream, down into the cellar room where they slept, so that my mother would grow up thinking she was just as good as the rich white daughter.

> If you white, you all right;
> if you brown, stick around;
> if you black, get back.

Somewhere the tables got turned, and the very ones who sang that song in their dark skins realized what they were singing, the ones who loved to comb and brush my "good" hair, and they blamed *us*.

Slowly I am changing, like something touched with love must change from the inside, like rot changes one, or the discovery of one's soul.

January

Last weekend we had the Wolfs over for dinner, friends we haven't seen since we lived in Hackensack. After we ate we were sitting having coffee in the living room—I had the stereo on—and I heard the crash of bottles outside. From where the noise was coming from, I surmised that the boy next door was having a party, his parents being out of town for the weekend.

About an hour later, there was a knock at the door. It was the police, who said that neighbors had complained about the noise. I was shocked and angry, outraged, and their accusation stirred those feelings of shame and guilt, as if I really *had* done something.

"Did you hear any noise when you came up to the door?" I asked, raising my voice.

"No," the policeman said.

"That's how it's been all night. We just have one couple over for dinner. What kind of noise could we be making?"

Tom Wolf is the police commissioner of a small town nearby. He came to the door, introduced himself, and showed his identification. He demanded to know which neighbor had complained and, maybe because he is the police commissioner, they begrudgingly told him. It was the Carters, an older couple on the block.

This morning, coming home from the grocery store, I saw Mrs. Carter pulling out of her driveway. I sped up, blocked her exit, and got out of my car.

"Last weekend I had a couple over for dinner and the police showed up at our door complaining that we were making noise. I have never been so embarrassed! They told us you complained." Her face became redder and redder. "The friend who was visiting is the police commissioner in Kenwood"—I wanted to let her know I have friends with some degree of power.

"Oh no," she burst out, more outraged than I was. "I didn't call the police about *you*, I would *never* call the police about *you*. *You're* the *black* family in the block!" It turned out that the Wicks' son had had a party, and the police had gone to the wrong house.

This afternoon flowers arrived at my door, spring flowers—tall forsythia and pussy willows—I'm sure a hundred dollars worth. I put them in a vase, smiling smugly, yet thinking I don't really deserve their guilt, as if what I have made them think about me weren't really true and, even if it were, there is still some false connection between the gift and the one who receives it. It just ended up with my name on it—"the black people on the block"—and I accept their pleasure and their pain.

August

Saturday morning Bruce and I spend a couple hours talking about the club. I want to try and join, to sue them, but I just don't have the energy and guts to do it without him. He says he's tired of talking about it. He tries to listen, but he's tired. He claims I'm taking this so hard because it's the first time I've directly felt the results of racism, the first time I've been refused because I'm black. I have never been refused service in a restaurant. And when I go into a store, the sales-person waits on me just as quickly as a white person. I don't get the constant reminders that people with dark skin grow so accustomed to that they are often not bothered. He says my color has given me a kind of mobility. The pain I feel now is the pain most black people experience when they are children, when they realize they cannot escape from their skin.

September

Tom gave me a Valium. We were at his house for dinner and talking about my fears, how I couldn't sleep. He is a drug salesman and he thought it would help me. I explained how I am terrified of pills. Since the time I smoked pot and had that paranoid and suicidal reaction, I never take anything, not even aspirin.

I took home two little pills in a brown medicine bottle. Last night I took one. I took a warm bath so that I would relax and asked Bruce to lie beside me until I went to sleep. I wanted him to guard me. I said, "During the night try to listen for me." When I was twelve I remember getting up during the night and trying to find the bathroom, though it was just across the hall. After a while I must have awakened my mother—"What are you doing?" "I can't find the bathroom," I said. I knew what I was doing, I was watching myself do it, but I couldn't stop myself. Could I kill myself during the night, run from the house, drive the car over a cliff without being able to feel myself? Bruce reassures me that he'll be there, and I lie down. Sure enough, a part of me lets go. I go down to my terrible dreams peacefully, taking them in like drinking impossible gulps of water.

This morning when I wake up, the dreams are just as present as they have ever been—those dreams of being washed in shit, as if my whole body, my whole self were nothing but shit, repulsive. I sit up in bed and put my feet over the side and something terrible and wonderful happens: I feel a weight, no, I can see it, a bar of steel like something you might see riding a flat car of a train coming over a part of my mind. I feel its cool weight descending, slowly pushing the shit-thoughts down, and it is not altogether a comforting feeling. So this is what repression is! Everywhere a shit-thought has been there is a sudden vacancy, a coldness like when the dentist shoots you with an anesthetic.

October

I can't bring myself to write. It is too painful. I sit in front of a blank sheet for hours. I can't remember. I don't want to say. What benefit can this be? It's already been done by somebody better. It's too late. Things have changed. Gotten better. Racism doesn't happen to people of my color, or to people with my degree of success, or education, or economic security. Light skin gives me such privileges that my complaints are not worthy. I'm not "positive" enough. Not "black" enough. I'm not a "real" black person. Worst of all are the terrible choices—the possibility of losing connections to those I love, betraying them, those who have done terrible things but at the same time have had to survive within the context of racism. Whose side am I on?

Once, after a reading, a white couple came up and told me that black people had done things to them, too. Did they think I was white and didn't like black people? Sometimes people can't get past what they think they see. Will my work give racists reasons? Then I felt the worst fear of all—that everything I have struggled for could be used to do the opposite of what I intended.

I think of Wordsworth's definition of poetry as "emotion recollected in tranquillity." This is not about memory. This is an act of destruction of the self, an undoing of the self's protection. Over and over I face the wall, the way in which I must confront my own complicity. Even the smallest fragment is a great victory.

"Forget" sounds like such a passive act, but anyone who has experienced the powerful force of repression will know the effort it takes to "unforget," to remember.

April

There is an article about me in a small paper. I am described as having "silky black hair that falls into my eyes" and "skin the color of pumpkin pie." What color is pumpkin pie?

The next day a white friend calls me. "How do you like being called the color of pumpkin pie?"

"Yeah," I say. "Isn't that crazy! What color *is* pumpkin pie?"

"Orange," she says. "That was so dumb . . . to say *anything* about color. If it was a white woman they wouldn't have said anything about color! And to say you are the color of pumpkin pie!"

The more she talked, the more I realized I *was* angry, furious; though yesterday, when I read the article, I had just laughed and shaken my head—"Well, I'm glad for the publicity," I had said to my husband.

It seems remarkably sad that it is a white woman's anger that makes me feel entitled to my own.

May

I had a dinner party last week. Saturday night, the first party in over a year. The house was dim and green with plants and flowers, light and orange, like a fresh fruit tart—openings of color in darkness, shining, the glass in the dark heart of the house opening out.

And I made sangria with white wine, adding strawberries, apples, oranges, limes, lemon slices, and fresh-squeezed juice in an ice-clear pitcher with cubes like glass lighting the taste with sound and texture.

And the table was abundant.

And they came: one man was a brilliant conversationalist, and his wife was happy to help in the kitchen; one woman was quiet and rigid as a fortress and black and stark as night, her brow a wall falling quickly, a swarthy drop, a steep incline away, and her husband was a doctor and introduced himself as "Doctor," and I said, "Charmed, Contessa Toinette." And we were black and white together, we were middle class and we had "been to Europe." And the doctors were black and the businessmen were white, and the doctors were white and the businessmen were black, and the bankers were there, too.

And the black people sat on this side of the room, and the white people sat on that, and they ate cherried chocolates with dainty fingers and told stories.

And soon I found that one belonged to Tall Oaks, and my heart closed, my eyes narrowed on that corner of the room, on that conversation like a beam of light. And they said, "Don't blame us; it's not our fault. It's the man who owns it." And I was angry and I said it *is* your fault for you belong and no one made you. And suddenly I wanted to belong. I wanted them to let me in or die. I wanted to go to court, to battle, to let crosses burn on my lawn, let anything happen. . . . *they will i will go to hell i will break your goddamned club apart don't give me shit anymore*

Bruce said it is illegal, and if we wanted to get in we could, no matter what the man at the top does. Everyone is blaming it on that one ugly man, and behind him they hide their ugliness, behind his big fat ass they hide their little house and little dishwasher, hide, like the Egyptians hid their children, hide their soaked brown evil smelling odor dripping ass, and they are saying, don't blame me, please, throwing up their hands, but I will not pass, like God, I will not pass over their evil.

The next day Bruce and I talk about it. He still doesn't want to pay the money to belong. He says it's not worth it. He doesn't want to fight to belong to something stupid; he would rather save his energy to fight for something important.

Important.

What is important to me?

No large goal like integrating a university. Just living on this cruddy street, taking it in my heart like an arrow.

August

I finally talked to my next-door neighbor, Mary, whose family has been here the longest, about some of the painful things that have happened since we moved here. I told her about my pain at not being asked to join the club—her husband is on the executive board—about our son being rejected by the kid up the street, about the woman coming to my house and saying, when she saw a picture of my mother's house, "I didn't know blacks had houses like this."

Thank God she didn't try to explain.

Thank God she didn't offer us dinner. When I finally talked to Ann—she never did invite us to the club—she invited us to their home for dinner, and we went, sick with anger but wanting to be forgiving. She poached salmon with crème fraîche and served it on her grandmother's china, with sterling and damask from Holland. I sat in the living room as sick as if I had eaten feces, my lips pulled back like a frightened dog.

I wanted to be far away, never to sit on her velvet chair, never to stand on her Oriental rug, never to see her kitchen floor with tiny suns and, in the back window, her cherry tree bursting out of the earth in two black joints. Never again let the kindness of a roof keep me from the truth of myself.

That night my heart touched self-hatred. It was as white as white light. It burned my eyes like a holocaust. I had to enter and be one with it before I could forgive myself.

Thank God Mary listened to me and expressed sadness. Thank God she said she didn't know my feelings had been hurt like this. She sat there as helpless as I am, innocent and guilty and sad.

December

This morning in our marriage counseling session, I bring up the estrangement I feel toward Bruce, for example, last night after making love. I had lain there with a terrible burden that I felt the need to share—that I often don't feel love for him or anyone! I had wanted so much to be in the warmth of our showering, soaping and oiling each other, kissing each other's bodies—but I felt outside, as if I had been in another woman's body. Then I remembered how just yesterday I had written about feeling superior to other blacks, feeling I am more intelligent, that I look better. I brought this up, saying that in some ways I think I am superior even to those I love, that I am better because I look white. Often black people I had intimate relationships with seemed to believe I was "better," too, from the time I was six and girls would fight over who would comb my "good" hair. In some way they took pride in it, as if it belonged to them, too!

I asked Bruce if he had married me because of my light skin, and he admitted that, partly, it was true. He was aware that my color, especially in business, would allow him to be seen in a different way.

Many times we have talked about how he grew up in an all-white town (there were two black families in the town and they lived side by side!), and was attracted to white girls. Fifty miles away, in Indiana, black boys were being lynched for just looking at a white woman, so his parents had made it very clear that he and his brothers were to put their energy into school and sports. "You have to be better than them," they always said. He remembers how, when he was nine, a neighbor commented to his father that he noticed Bruce had stopped smiling.

I have always thought Bruce was the one person in the world who loved me for myself. We have been married for twenty years and never talked about color. Now I see I am partly a shield he is holding up for protection. He, too, has a secret in the corner of his heart that stands between us like a mirror we don't want to look into.

I tell him how, when we pull up in front of a hotel, I want to rush out of the car door, to go in before him just in case he will be given an inferior room. Often I don't because I don't want him to be "emasculated," not to have the normal power of a male to get a hotel room, but I distrust what women are supposed to trust in their men—this power of acquisition—I often feel I could do better alone. Then I say the terrible thing I have never been able to say, that sometimes when I look at his color and the shape of his nose, I feel revulsion.

I feel so sad, so frightened! That I should feel these feelings! What is love? And he says something even more terrifying and sad—that he doesn't blame me, often when he looks in the mirror, he can't stand his own ugly face. I remember how his mother wouldn't let him go out without white powder, how he slept in a stocking cap for years after we married. There is a long silence in which we just sit there in the hell of Bruce's agony. There is nothing to say.

After therapy we stand outside together beside our cars. We don't touch, yet we don't seem to want to go our separate ways. We don't say anything for a long time, then I joke—because I can't speak seriously about the terrible things we've told each other—"So you wanted to marry a white woman?" "Yes," he answers, as if he has no energy left to play.

We stand like this for a long time. I still don't feel "love," but I do feel a kind of tenderness, a desire to go with him and put my hand on his sad, beautiful face.

We lived there for six years. We were never invited to join the club and our neighbors never took us there for dinner. My anger and sense of isolation turned into fury and dislocation. We decided to move—and moved to another all-white community—but this time into a house from which I couldn't see our neighbors' houses on either side. I had given up on the hope of neighborhood friendships. During those years I had become more established as a poet, and my friends had become the people whose values I shared. My husband's friends continued to be men with whom he did business. Our son went to boarding school. I heard that one of our neighbors moved to Florida, that the husband of one of the young women died of a brain tumor and she moved to another state. I haven't visited since the day I moved away, but I have heard that many of the same families remain. The last I heard the club is still all white.

Blacks
in the U.

I will place a new heart
within you.

Isaiah

There is a new black woman in the English department. Several people told me about her, that she is extremely nice, and that she looks white—like me. The way they described her, I didn't know what I'd see, though I think I thought to myself, *Another "nice" light-skinned girl who knows how to make people like her.* I thought, *Well, I guess either I've done a great job and they've decided they can get along with light-skinned black women, or well, here is the light-skinned black woman who is <u>still</u> nice, the one coming to take my place.*

I was sitting in a colleague's office and a nice-looking young woman stuck her head in the door. My colleague introduced us, *This is the new person on staff.* She was so happy to meet me, I realized this must be the young woman I had heard so much about—the brilliant, sweet, pleasant, lovely, new black woman who looks white. I suddenly had that feeling that I was looking at her through something—that I had backed up fifty yards to stare at her through a pinhole. Either she was showing something or I was seeing something so much in contrast to what I wanted to see that I didn't want to see it.

I was (1) seeing if she really *did* look white, (2) seeing if she looked as white as *me*, (3) saying, *She's young, beautiful, charming, I'm on the way out*, (4) and I was in love with her, too —she is graceful, (5) saying, *She's nice to me now, but I will soon let her down*, (6) saying, *She's trying to get something from me, she'll use me, hurt me*, (7) thinking, *Oh my god, they've brought in another one. Then, I really <u>am</u> here, not because of me, but because that's the only skin they can tolerate.* And I thought how sad it is that we *are* here, either because we *are* the only people they can find or because they want us to be. I felt despairing and helpless.

When I was having lunch with her, all the feelings persisted, the fears and attractions. And I realized that something rare had happened when I saw her.

Often, when I see a black person, after having been in an all-white environment like this one for a long time, I experience a kind of shock, as if I've forgotten I'm black and seeing that person makes me remember. It often comes upon me with a feeling of dread and repulsion, as if I'm looking in a mirror I don't want to see, and I have great shame about these feelings. But when I realized *she* was black, I felt another kind of distancing—the shock of recognizing what *I* look like. I said to myself, *So <u>this</u> is what it is to look white to others.* I felt a kind of disbelief, a lack of trust, as if something about her were deliberately deceitful and I had to watch out. And then I felt great fear for myself, for how I must be judged.

I have written about that sudden feeling of distance and alienation when I see a dark person which has so disturbed me. I had thought if I acknowledged it, told the truth, if I admitted how racism has been internalized, then that awful feeling would go away. I had thought that that reaction was connected to seeing someone dark, a dark man, for that is the image I thought we had been taught mostly to hate and fear. But now I see that if you are black, there is no skin to be safe in, that that moment of separation and fear can be attached to anyone, that sometimes it is a honey-colored woman or even a child, that just as there is an internalized picture of a hated and feared dark person, there is also a picture of a hated and feared light woman, and she looks like *me.* Perhaps there are even deeper structures than racism that keep us from touching the most fearful aspects of our own natures. Perhaps my "other" is *me.*

She did seem well-mannered, considerate, kind, and quick to help. When a waiter broke a glass, she bent down immediately to help him pick up the broken pieces. Instead of thinking, *How kind she is,* I thought, *She's just trying to impress me.* Or, *Why didn't I think to do that?*

Later, we exchanged mother stories and talked about the difficulty of separating, especially of establishing ourselves as our own women, assuming our sexual lives. She is trying to live on her own, to be separate from her mother, and it is very hard, since for years her mother was her best friend. I could tell she feels a great deal of sadness and fear about these changes. I told her that the first thing my mother had said to me when I was born was, *I will never be alone again.* And how, when I went home this last time and tried to be that "Toi" who entertained my mother, the sweet, funny, good girl, telling funny stories and gossiping, I couldn't do it. (My poor mother, who thought my love would replace the love of the mother who had died when she was eighteen; and me, the poor daughter of a woman who took every hint of separation as a betrayal.) I knew that eventually the old partings would come, and that that sudden and terrifying feeling of disappointment and separation would come over me, making me doubt the very root of love. I told her that what I grieved for most was not the relationship with my mother, but the part of me that couldn't go back and be that thing that had tried so hard to please her, to stay connected, the part that now felt so distant and guarded, so isolated and strange. *Who am I if I am not the one I used to be?*

It's funny. Seeing her begins with race and color and ends with us talking about our mothers, about separating and being a grown-up, and I wondered if that great grief of separation is connected to all these other moments of space between us—even the spaces of race and color.

Sometimes I think that eventually every identity breaks down to some self that has to learn to live between loneliness and connection, stuck in some primal way. I think of the terror of being alone. I don't mean that being black can ever be a lost identity in this racist world, or that it should be. I don't mean anything like, "I don't see color," as some people say. But that in some way even our connections to the ones most like us become unsolid, unreal, and though there is a necessity for trust and commitment, in another way we are nothing more than some kind of spirit-movement walking through the world clothed in a story of our life.

Perhaps this revulsion for the other is really a revulsion for my own self, my own fears of being "other," separate and alone. Perhaps accepting this distance, even from the ones most like me, the ones I love and would like to be closest to, is really the way I will finally see us as we truly are, all of us "other," frighteningly distant from each other, and yet needing and loving each other.

I remember a game I used to play in childhood; it was one of my favorite games and I played it for years. I would put myself in my grandmother's pantry behind the gate where they locked the dog, and I'd play "elevator," closing the gate, going up, opening. I may have been enacting a fear, for my grandmother was terrified of elevators and wouldn't go into a store or building if that was the only way she could go up, and it has been a fear of mine, too. For years I wouldn't get on a plane, and I was terrified of being on a bridge that was crowded and not being able to get off, of being somewhere, anywhere, where I couldn't have access to something, somebody who loved me, who would save me from feeling alone. The anxiety was unbearable. I couldn't stand to be cut off and left to my own feelings of distance and terror.

I hear the dogs whining next door. Maybe they are locked up. I think of but can't imagine that feeling of being shut away again and again, weeping and begging, humiliated and in incredible pain, and going through it every day, every day forgetting what it felt like and coming out and loving those same people again, as if every day the part that loves is regenerated and then torn off again, like people coming back to live the same life over and over, and you can see it from a distance and know that every day they are going to have to live that same pain.

Or perhaps being alone you make up your mind to like it, to be in there thinking or talking to yourself or looking out the window or making up a game or a poem, and suddenly you're glad you're alone, you don't want them to come anywhere near you, and you feel that only if you're alone can you have your own life, write your own poetry, think, be, and hating the fact that maybe they might want you, call you, expect you to pay attention.

And then starting to like being with them, starting to trust that they can listen to you, that you can orchestrate the space between you so that you don't feel destroyed, taken advantage of. You can do it the other way, you can have your own separate and isolated life, but still, for a moment, here, it almost feels as if someone understands you and you understand that person, and you begin to think, well, why not want everything different, why not begin a new way, and you think, well now, maybe forever.

Race isn't a metaphor. Color isn't a metaphor. It doesn't feel like a metaphor. It hurts as if it's my skin. I feel sick. I hate myself. I make you hate me. I separate. I come back. Forgive me. This is the best I can do.

What I discovered when I saw the other white-looking woman in my colleague's office was that I loved her, was that going down into any "other"—as I might now be able to go down into my own self's "otherness" —I find everything intact I was made to put out of me. Not just the dark person but the light one, too, and the colors between, and the too fat and the too skinny and the frightening, dangerous father, and the weak, depressed one, and the huge white God with his head like a smokestack, and the beaten dog, and the mother scrubbing the tub with a rag, and the grandmother in her quilted death, and the other mother with her long black hair braided on top of her head like a tiara, and the poor boy standing over me with a knife who stank of pee and nearly took my life, and my own beautiful son, and my gold grandson, and the white and black of what we have all been called, and, even deeper, that blank moment of nothingness and separation that I fear more than my own death.

Never show your fear, my father always said when we'd see a big dog, *they can smell it.* But it is fear that I have acknowledged and taken in.

The Thought

A black graduate student has just moved into an apartment building in which all of the other three tenants are white. Last week one of the tenants mentioned to him—"in passing," he reports, "completely without emphasis, really almost as an oversight," and he is almost sure of that—that a bike belonging to one of the other tenants had been stolen. It had happened a couple of weeks before. Certainly they didn't suspect him. If they had suspected him, they wouldn't have waited two weeks to say something. He was sure that his neighbors weren't trying to make him feel guilt or apprehension. He was sure that the man was saying it just as he would have said it to any other neighbor. He didn't sense in the least that there was any kind of accusation.

Immediately after, however, the thought kept going around in his head—what if he *had* done it? What if he just didn't remember? What if the bike was up there right now in his room? And he remembered how, another time, at a party where he was the only black person, a white woman had said that there was a dollar missing from her purse, and though nobody looked at him, he grew silent and withdrew, and he kept thinking, almost believing, that it was *he* that *was* the thief, that the dollar was right there in his pocket, that if they would just look in his wallet, it would be there. He could feel it in his back pocket burning into his skin, and he was sure that if he pulled out his wallet and opened it, the dollar would leap out, searing like a coal.

He thought about the bike for days, wondering how he had done it, where he had put it. Then, one day, getting into his car, he thought, why would I steal a bike? I don't need a bike, I have a car. And, just that quickly, the thought disappeared.

Letter to an Editor Who Wants to Publish a Black Writer

Dear —,

I read your letter over today and something struck me. You say about my second book, concerning the birth of my son in a home for unwed mothers: "Your conversation with your own body in *Natural Birth* is so brave and important—the spliced dangers that come with color, with young, single motherhood and with the weight of medical abuse for women, especially women of color—all of that speaks very powerfully." It was interesting to me because, in this case, every other woman in that book was white. I hate the fact that knowing a writer is black changes the meaning of everything he or she writes. I am always being fitted into what is expected. It makes me furious because I keep having this added burden and responsibility, not only to tell *my* truth but also to write in such a way that it compensates for what's in people's heads. If I don't, even in *your* case, a sophisticated, well-meaning, and sensitive reader, people superimpose a context quite inaccurate that completely overwhelms, even destroys, what I have created. I have worked so hard to create a certain meaning, to control meaning. It makes me furious that other meanings, ones that I have no control over, are the ones through which my work is read.

I don't know if my son's birth in a home for unwed mothers had anything to do with my being black. Perhaps I *was* treated differently than the other girls, though, frankly, I had only told the social workers I was black. I never did tell the girls, the nuns, or the doctors, so, maybe, they didn't know.

Another confusing thing is that perhaps, even though I don't perceive it, I am *always* writing about a "black" experience because I *am* black. Maybe no matter what I write about, no matter what I say or don't say, even if I am writing about a situation in which race is not important and/or stated, I am writing in a way that is recognizably different from that of a white person's—because blackness is at the center of everything I do.

I remember doing a reading this summer at a small, nearby college. It was a very successful reading, and one of the things that pleased me most was that the black students seemed to sense I was black even though I never read a poem that specifically said so. Perhaps there is something deeper that I am not aware of.

The thing that makes me sad and furious is when people see my work in one way and then, suddenly, when they find out I'm black, begin to ascribe all kinds of meanings that are stereotypical—for example, assuming that the pregnant, unmarried girls in my book must be black. Perhaps that's why I don't like to write about racial issues. I hope not to be locked into those terrible, narrow places that seem to become more and more impossible to extricate one-self from.

To be published as a "woman of color" makes me squiggle on a pin: I want to be read by white people, and not just white people who are interested in "black" writing. I want even my speaking about color to speak in some universal way.

Yesterday, at my office, the woman in the travel agency wanted to know what I am. "Are you Egyptian?" No, I answered, and I said how pleased I was that she would ask me that because people who have visited that part of Africa have told me I look like someone from there. (To myself, "I am so happy—it is really true that I have a claim to that home!") But when she asked again, I said "mixed." Consciously I chose not to say black. I want to be invisible in my office, to go and come without that tension of being the only different one.

I was raised to think class was the issue. If we drove around in a Mercedes, if we had clothes from Saks, if we were doctors, if we were light-skinned, things would be different. But there is always the rub. Recently my cousin, a doctor, was stopped in his new Mercedes in a white suburb and taken to jail because he didn't have plates yet.

I remember the time I was attacked. A black man ran up alongside my car and I remember thinking, *Don't lock your door. It will show you don't trust black men.* Then, just as now, I tried to prove that point, just as when I brought home dark men to prove I wasn't like those in my family who said it took four generations to get us the color we are and they didn't want me messing things up.

When the man pulled my car door open and fell on me, I smelled him, the agony in him, the urine in his crib, the sweat of terror that had dried inside him and could never be washed away. The hatred of the whole world fell on me like vomit. I would have killed or died to stop that one instant in which his smell entered me.

"Don't scream," he said, and I started to scream, to do exactly the opposite of whatever he told me.

"I'll kill you," he said.

"You're going to have to kill me," I said.

"Who said that?" I asked myself, suddenly realizing it was too late to take it back, that I had to stand in for the one who said that.

I grabbed the blade of the knife he was holding and fought him off. Finally, he stood up, wiped the blood off the blade, and casually walked away. "Bitch," he called back. And did I hear him say, "I always knew you light-skinned bitches were like that!"

That is the worst accusation—that my color is near proof that I don't love my people enough to suffer the consequences of their anger toward me, their abuse. It doesn't matter how much I try to prove I am not what they think, there is a deeper part far beyond my control that *is.*

No, of course he didn't say that. There is no way he could have known. Still, I know he is the one that we have, for four generations, fucked and climbed to get away from.

I think of my mother when she was three years old, on the train with her mother, going to the rich white people's house where her mother would be cook. She was leaving her father behind in that alley where they had lived, in a house with no address. And she was so excited that she felt no sadness. Even now she says, "I don't want to talk about the painful." What agony in the moment when one chooses the train away from one's deepest attachments. What pain one turns from and what pain one turns to!

I know I have the right to protect myself, to lock the door when a black or white man runs up beside my car, to go to the best college, to try to get published by the best (white?) publishers, but there is that moment: the breaking of the self in two.

A Woman Who Looks White

The woman on the TV talk show looks white, is confident, unerring, and unashamed of herself; but the audience doesn't believe she is black, not the blacks or the whites, and they are all angry that she has dyed her hair blond. They accuse her of dating whites, though she says, and I believe, that she has never dated whites. Her attitude is tough: "I know I'm black, and I don't care what you think of me." She is definitely not sucking up to any of them.

The blacks and the whites are allied in their hatred. Perhaps the whites are mad because they don't want to think that anyone who looks as white as they do could be black. They don't want the lines to be fuzzy. And perhaps they are mad because they feel betrayed. If somebody who *could* be one of them doesn't want to be, maybe being white isn't as great as they thought. And many blacks have worked hard not to want to *be* that woman. The irritant might creep under the door. Some of us, without thinking, may still refer to her "good" hair.

Several young men at an all-black college recently told me that in their dreams they saw themselves as colorless or white. Sometimes a sin in thought, even if uncommitted, is just as stinking. When we look at her we remember that somebody made somebody else feel like shit and then preferred the world that way. The thing that we don't confess is that a part of us also believes in some shit-list universe, a club where we can sit with others who don't have the dung of their own being on their hands.

If she had been white, her self-possession under attack may have been admirable. But for a black woman—and a light-skinned black woman at that, who should at least be sorry for her color—to be so imperturbable, to have gotten away with her own self-worth . . . well, it seemed totally wrong, as if she had gotten away with murder.

She shows photographs of relatives from several generations back, all of whom look like the most middle-class people from Iowa—men in business suits, educators, lawyers, doctors, ministers, and women with fluffy soft hair and a sense of security in their eyes. It is as if the family built a city around her heart which had protected her from what we are all supposed to suffer, as if she hadn't yet heard the news.

By the time I was in second grade, I already knew that white people had something special, desirable, a world I wanted to enter. On the first day of school, when the nun put the index card on my desk on which we were to neatly pen our names and addresses, and check the one appropriate box—Negro or White—I hesitated as long as I could. Was it a test to see if I'd lie? Though both my parents look white, could they know because of something one of them had said? Could I leave it blank? I had a sense that checking "Negro" would mean I would become something confusing. Perhaps later they would read the card and think I had made a mistake—why wouldn't they think I was white? But they taught us that the eye of God sees all. "Negro," I finally checked.

In third grade Susan, the teacher's pet, had long red hair and green eyes. She treated the other children the way certain dogs treat others when their owners explain, "He thinks he's human." She was always the one who took Sister Ann's messages to the office, always the one to mark on the blackboard the names of the children who talked when she was gone—the one sent, the one left in charge and trusted. What was inside a girl who had such power? Perhaps it was what made white people live in different neighborhoods. I tried to talk to her in line, but she never succumbed. I tried to talk to her at lunch, but there was absolutely nothing she needed.

She had a cousin in our class, Catherine, a girl whose clothes were always too ruffly, too large on her thin body, so that they shifted constantly into the position of a hand-me-down. Susan waited for her after school each day and walked her to the bus with the air of noblesse oblige. In the class picture, Catherine's thin face strains toward the camera with a trying smile. Under her closed lips are teeth with little gold-black holes. My mother was ferocious about good teeth and feet. Something was going wrong inside that it was already too late to fix.

One afternoon Catherine invited me to her house for dinner. I didn't know there were apartments over storefronts, entrances on the sides of buildings, doors that put you in front of long, narrow stairways where you could smell things cooking. I had never opened a door into a living room with bare floors and several cribs in a row against the far wall, one with a toddler in it laughing and reaching for us. I could smell pee in her house—*pee!* There was a beat-up dinner table and things out of place. When it was time for dinner, there was stew from a can, and everyone sat down as if it was a special treat because I had come. It was stringy and tasteless. I ate one tiny forkful at a time.

I remember the cruel pride I felt bringing her to my house, the beef stroganoff I had asked my mother to make, the paintings and music. I don't think she even noticed what I was trying so hard to prove—white people are so often completely oblivious to the twisted worlds that have been swept out of their way. I think she just wanted to be my friend.

That night I was terrified when it was time for her father to pick her up. What would he say when he saw his daughter standing out in front of my building? I made her walk up to the corner, even though it was raining, because I thought at least there he might see Mr. Fadell, the white man who owned the corner market.

Then I understood that there was a factor that could turn being black into something quite comfortable, and turn being white into a bad fate. There were no absolutes, though to Catherine's father, and to most white people, such distinctions would be inconceivable.

Recently a white friend defended private clubs by saying, "But even *I* couldn't get into some clubs." He was willing to take for granted his own unworthiness by certain clubs' standards, but he could not conceive that some black person could be perfectly worthy by the same standards that would keep him out. Once a dear white friend said to me when I got a job that she had applied for, "Why didn't *I* get that job?" Competition between friends is hard enough, but when there is an underlying belief that all blacks are just getting ahead because of your kindness, then losing out makes it much rougher. Sometimes some black person has jokingly said, "It's for very few white folks and no niggers." It isn't some bottom line of accessibility that blacks want to attain, some common denominator that most white people take for granted. The dizzying complexity of class means that while we have been as handicapped by the rules as a swimmer with both hands tied behind her back, we stuck to them and, dammit, since we stuck to them, we are determined to have it all: schools, clubs, money, power—what very few white people and no niggers have.

I remember thinking how happy Catherine's family seemed, how much more accepting and lenient with their children. The thought occurred to me that perhaps white people, being without the stresses that race brings into their family, might be easier to live with, might be more accepting of me than my own people.

Sometimes my mother would drop me off at Heather Martin's. I knew it was my big chance. It would make my mother happy. You kept going up and up in her house to a special room made of wood like an attic, a playroom full of stuffed animals and dollhouses. For years, every time I went home my mother would say, "Heather keeps asking about you!" Finally, I called her. It was dinnertime, and after forty years of silence, she said her lamb chops were burning. I was fifty. A fifty-year-old woman yelling at her mother, "Don't you ever mention that girl again!" And my mother miserably said, "But I never cared if the two of you were friends!"

But she *did* care.

Until my parents were divorced, they were always invited to the Christmas Eve open house. My aunt and uncle dropped them off, my mother in a strapless "eveling" gown, as I used to call it, her long black hair braided like a tiara across her head, my father tall and handsome. They let me peak in the door at the table in the huge foyer with a crystal bowl heaped with whipped cream—"You had to eat it with a spoon!" my mother said. Silver trays of pretty little foods, mirrors, polished marble floors, fire, chandelier, and the brilliant tree. My mother was grateful and slightly feverish, and my father put on his dashing act, joking with the men and flattering the women endearingly.

There was an "in" and an "IN" in the upper class, and we very well knew the difference. Some of the men were respected doctors, their wives did good civic work, but they weren't called every day with the gossip. Beauty could not get you in—or my mother and father would have been first in line—not money, or family, or profession, not even the number of generations in the city—though being an "old Detroiter" was very important. Where you lived was very important, and what color you were, but most important was whom you married. My mother's chances got slimmer and slimmer as her marriage failed, for it was almost certain that you came, if you were a woman, with a certain kind of man.

Shortly after I was born, my mother took the two thousand dollars' inheritance that my grandmother had left her and paid for my father to go to Chicago to Worsham Embalming School. She had hoped he would join his stepfather in the family business, "Webster's Funeral Home." Each week she would pick up the oppressive and inadequate five dollars' "help" that "Budd" Webster would hand to her in an envelope out of the Cadillac window. She was working downtown. My aunt had gotten her a job, as she had done for so many of the women in my family, in the mail room of Annis Furs, where she was the supervisor. Every Wednesday my mother would wait after my grandfather's call for fifteen minutes before she went out, even pregnant and in snow, so that he wouldn't have to park.

We lived with my aunt and uncle until I was seven in Conant Gardens, one of the first black middle-class suburbs of Detroit—a quiet neighborhood with perfect lawns. At one time all the black people had lived together in "Blackbottom." Many of the cream-colored had floated away to mansions on Arden Park and Boston Boulevard. We were stuck in the middle, post office workers, teachers, and social workers.

Often, when relatives were visiting from out of town, we'd drive through the crowded streets of Blackbottom on Saturday night, to laugh at those loud people, to be as close to them as we could allow ourselves, to envy them and to think we were better—the drunks and prostitutes, the sweating women with their steel drums of barbecue cooking on the streets. Then we'd drive through the fancy boulevards, the neighborhoods of those people who sometimes invited my aunt and mother to showers and meetings of the bridge club.

Once a year my aunt and my mother cooked for days. They'd decorate the house with flowers, the whole house, even the bathroom with a small bouquet of a hundred violets that I had picked from the side of the house and arranged in my grandfather's gold antique shaving mug. They put on dark red silk, gold, and pearls. They rouged their cheeks. In ironed aprons they served shrimp salad in little crispy pastry shells. They put paprika in cream cheese and stuffed celery and tomatoes; they cupped rice in teacups so that it stood in perfect mounds on a huge flowered platter with a nip of parsley on top of each. If Aunt Edith came, she brought a coconut cake three stories high that almost floated off the china. People passed through the kitchen and filled their plates until they were heavy, joking about what good cooks my mother and my aunt were.

If it had been up to my mother, she would have done it. She would have worked twenty hours a day. But it wasn't up to a woman. And for my father, that five-dollars-a-week salary that his stepfather had offered him was the last straw. Once, when his mother and stepfather were sitting out on their front porch, my father raced by in the red Porter's Cleaner van without waving or even looking their way. His stepfather had run out to the street and called to him. Then he threw his hat down and stomped on it. "That's the end," he had proclaimed.

Still, my father could have made it. He could have used his beauty, his color, his charm. Long after everyone had given up on him, there was still his old friend Rad, one of the wealthiest and most loved members of old society, who took him to Mexico on vacation, who spoke lovingly on the phone to my mother about "holding on." My father was gravitating toward people whom he called "the real people," toward that woman who didn't pick up his ashtray every time he put a cigarette down.

When I was two, my mother was pregnant again, with the child they hoped to be his boy. She had almost died of toxemia with me, and yet she had to try again. All the women were obligated to try a second time if they hadn't gotten it right the first. She swelled up like a tire, black, and couldn't get into her shoes. She waded around inside herself trying to bend and scrub the floor, lift the water-heavy clothes and put them through the wringer. Then there was blood down the basement stairs and my mother was crying. They left me off at Aunt Blanche's, where I sat awake all night, frightened. Several days later I waved at my mother from the hospital parking lot. She was up in the window without her baby.

In Conant Gardens we made a world of perfect

lawns, lily ponds, huge blue spruces, fields where you could still find walking sticks and, on the milkweed pods, red bugs that sang when we cupped them gently in our hands, the cleared fields from which jutted the bones of new houses, Mr. Rucker's "ark," painted red, white, and blue, and Cunningham's Sweet Shop.

We ate salmon croquettes or tuna fish and chips on Fridays. Pot roast, fried chicken breasts, okra gumbo, and upside-down cake on Sunday; Mass at Holy Ghost, Detroit's first black Catholic church, in a cool basement, whose red-haired, thick-in-the-middle Irish priest sometimes consoled my mother with a hug; my aunts and my mother in their slips in the kitchen with beer and Chinese food, laughing loudly or whispering conspiratorially about those no-good men. At two, I proclaimed my allegiance: "The only thing a man is good for is to go to the 'tore,' and even then he comes back with the wrong thing."

On winter nights, my Aunt Lenora would come home after dark. My mother would have covered her dinner with wax paper and put it on the back burner. I'd be waiting at the door for my surprise—colored paper, a sharpened pencil, a book with pretty pictures, or, if she had forgotten, a dirty Tum dug from the bottom of her purse. She called it "candy," which made it taste good. She'd eat standing at the sink and then we'd sneak out from the troubles of that house.

In the windows of colored Conant Gardens, the people were lit up like saints. The old man in the moon with his battered and benign face followed us. I'd wish on the first star, a silent wish—that all my family would be happy—my hand stuffed like a sausage in the pocket of her warm "burr" coat.

Among
School
Children

*The death of a child is the
greatest reason to doubt
the existence of God.*

<small>DOSTOYEVSKY</small>

Teachers Workshop

This morning I did a teachers workshop in a small town—just about 99.44 percent "pure." I explained how I have the children write poems using oxymorons: "Think of something you can see very clearly, or feel very strongly. Now think of its opposite. Like—*Sun. Cold sun.* Or—*Rainbow. Black rainbow.*" One teacher said, "That's negative thinking. I don't like negative thinking. I want my rainbows to be colored good colors. Pretty colors. Not black. I don't like all this negative thinking." Immediately another teacher chimed in. "Yes. And what has happened to meter and rhyme?"

My stomach knotted up. They've found out what I am, what I bring to this lily-white happy town. Not that they know I'm black. But something subtle and unseen. There is something I know that they don't want to know, something that comes out of my blackness. I bring the dreaded disease. I encourage their children to open their hearts to the "dark" side. To know the fear in them. To know the rage. To know the repression that has lopped off their brains just as it has lopped off the brains of the children in the ghetto, only theirs is a painless death, the victims so anesthetized they don't kick.

Lightning Bug

I asked the children to do a self-portrait with words. One girl, a black girl, Alicia, didn't like the way she looked. I told her that for everything she named that she didn't like about herself, I would name one thing I didn't like about myself.

She named teeth.

I named stomach.

She named fat.

I named feet.

She named hair. She named skin. This little girl in the second grade thinks she is ugly because of her hair and skin. She said the only pretty girl in class is Tracy—the white girl.

I sat down next to her and told her how, when I was in second grade, all the girls were drawing pictures of white women—movie stars—and saying when they grew up they wanted to look like them. I asked her if she understood what I was saying. She said I was trying to tell her that she would never be white.

I told her yes, in a way I was saying that.

Another girl in class said if you were going to a Black Muslim school, you would think white people were ugly.

I told Alicia that she *was* beautiful, her hair, her eyes, her skin, her nose. I told her the most beautiful thing about her is the energy inside her which is so full and bright it bursts out as if she has a lightning bug inside. She wrote this poem:

My name is Alicia.
Mrs. Derricotte thinks I'm pretty.
She says I have a lightning bug inside me.
And that makes me smile.

Baby Pictures

I had asked the fourth graders to bring in baby pictures. I was going to play a game with them: have them guess which picture belonged to which fourth grader, talk about being a baby, and write. That morning, as the children mixed their pictures in a pile, the face of the only black girl in the room came at me with new clarity. I sensed this game might put her in danger.

The children fumbled over several pictures, guessing, "Tracy?" "Sharon?" When I held up Deborah's picture, they didn't hesitate. "That's Deborah," they said in unison.

Deborah looked shocked. "How did they guess me so fast?" She looked hurt, as if she had been discovered in a good hiding place. "How did they know it was me?"

Either the children didn't consciously know or else they were ashamed to say. One girl said, "You can tell by her brother standing next to her."

I thought of the way Deborah sits in the last seat, in the last row, as far back as possible, still she sticks out like a sore thumb. "That's Deborah," they had all said in unison.

Her face fell in disbelief. She came up to look at the picture, trying to discern what had given her away. She held it up, turning it, talking to herself, "But how did they know that was my brother?"

Clarissa

My friend Mady said how disturbed she was about racial problems in the small town she's teaching in. The community is largely white and upper middle class. However, there is a poor black section. Many of the mothers in this section are maids in the households of other children in the school. In each class there is one black child, and this child is also outstanding in terms of behavior. In one class, the girl is superbright, super personality; in another the girl is the slowest. When asked to write something about her hand, she wrote: "My hand is clean." The teacher said, "That girl comes to school every day smelling and dirty." In the other classrooms, the black children are either the clowns or the "bad" kids, almost all of them far behind. When Mady talked to teachers, they looked at her like she was crazy. "There's no racism here!"

I remember Clarissa, that girl who came to school each day starched and pressed all over—her kinky curls, her pinafore. I think of her oiled, gold skin, her knobby knees and thin calves like a filly's. She always talked at the wrong time, stood up at the wrong time, had to go to the bathroom. "Clarissa, didn't you go when the other children went?" And no matter how clean she was when her mother sent her, no matter how many times she brought home bad reports, each day Clarissa screamed as if crazy.

I think of the teacher lifting her, screaming, away from the dollhouse where the other girl whines, "She's taking my doll," holding her kicking feet away, carrying her down the hall at arm's length to the office, as if she had the plague. Clarissa screams for her body lifted against her will, screams because her mother will beat her, screams because she will sit all morning in the window of the principal's office where everyone will see.

How did this happen? By first grade it is already too late, and in spite of her mother, who spent her maid's paycheck on a white pinafore so that Clarissa would fit in, she *doesn't* fit in, and her mother isn't strong enough to beat that devil out of her.

What makes Clarissa jump out of her skin?

Kin

A black boy in the fourth grade says to me, "I'd like to be your son."

A white boy sitting near him responds, "You could *never* be her son."

"Why not?" I ask.

"Because he's black."

"But I'm black, too."

He looks at me, his eyes swimming with confusion and pain.

White children might have a more difficult time forming a concept of kinship with people of different colors. Black children grow up in families where there is every conceivable color, texture of hair, thickness of feature. In white families there is much less difference. I decide to test this.

"How many in the room have people in their family that are all different colors, some people as light as I am, some people as dark as Sheldon?"

All the black kids raise their hands.

"How many have people in their family that are all just about the same color?"

All the white kids raise their hands.

Schools with predominantly white children want to teach the concept of the human family by including pictures of black people in texts. But valuing the other, learning we are all the same blood, is not a lesson one learns with the mind.

There was an article in *The New York Times* about a black woman, an actress, who was hired to go to an all-white school in Iowa so that the kids could get to see and talk to a black person. Among the thousand students, none were black. Before she went onstage, she walked through the audience and let them touch and hug her. She held out her hands to them and let them crowd around her.

I once said you are black because of who you first love, the first people whose skin you touched. Yet being black seems so much larger than touch, so much more invisible than body. My aunt used to say, "If you to talk to yourself, it's OK, as long as you don't answer." Being black happens when one is utterly alone.

The other night we had several friends over, and the conversation turned to our experiences as black people. We talked politics, neighborhood, business, and then started talking family. We were talking about that part of being black that is private and that we want to protect. One woman said she felt invaded when she went to *for colored girls who have considered suicide/when the rainbow is enuf* and saw all the white people in the audience. Somehow she felt like we were giving up our secrets, like, somehow, we would become vulnerable and be taken advantage of by white people if they were shown the cracks in our image, as if they were witch doctors who had captured our toenails, a strand of our hair, or our feces. Another friend talked about how she just zips into her white skin whenever the occasion calls for it, and she feels very comfortable about it. No problem. Then, when she gets with black people, she just zips off her white skin and zips into her black.

I started talking about my fears for my son, who is growing up so differently than I grew up. When I was young, all my friends, all my family's friends, all my family were black; maybe their skin wasn't black, but they all identified themselves as black. Everyone I touched, everyone who touched me, everyone I loved was black inside their heart, and whatever made them black—even if it wasn't their skin—was there all the time I was feeling love and rage for them.

How little my son has that will give him that sense of connection. Tony has mostly white friends over to spend the night. We have been cut off from our family in Detroit since we moved East, isolated like an island floating in an almost all-white sea. We never belonged to any church. Our belief in religion wasn't strong enough to get us up every Sunday morning, and I felt like a liar for trying to build a community of religion when my own belief was so unsure. There were no relatives whose house he could sleep over in, curling in their bed, touching his head inside their warm arm. Just us, his mother and father, and the world outside. We hoped he'd learn love. But what of those deep roots? Where will his strength come from? I have my strength in my black roots, my life deep in my belly, like warm stew. Where will his roots be, to hang on to when the wind shakes him, after I am gone?

We talked for hours. I was not the only one; in varying degrees, we all have problems. Some kids go to private schools, or mostly white schools. We are injected into the white community and it is injected into us.

After the conversation, I thought, this is what being black is. This conversation here tonight about our pains, our griefs, our sadnesses, our triumphs. This conversation with this great energy and this great depth in our hearts. I have been mistaken in thousands of groups for white, and I have taken part in conversations that touch on things deep and personal with white people. But I cannot conceive of white

Burn Victim

Visiting a friend in the hospital, I took a tour around the neighboring pediatric unit. There was a little black boy around three years old walking about encased in a gauze sarcophagus, only his face visible, a little sausage twirl at the top of his head. He walked forward stiffly, his arms braced in the air by metal bars, like a little Frankenstein.

He didn't smile, but pushed an empty stroller as if it were the most normal thing in the world. His tiny face peered out, unsuspicious, full of gentle acquisitiveness.

A nurse came along and took his arm. "Time for apple juice and bed." She guided him to the nurses' station, and he didn't cry as she pulled him along, not so gently, his feet hurrying, padded thickly, trying to keep up.

Deep inside me flashed this shame: often when I see a black child, the crime of the skin blazes up before me, a feeling passes over me like a flush, and I hold myself separate. This happens so quickly that no one knows—and, in fact, it is such a painful knowledge that, most frequently, I myself do not realize it. My mind thinks instantly past the barrier, and I am kind— perhaps overly kind—to make up for it.

In this case, I felt nothing but sorrow. And my mind contrasted my past feelings with what I felt now. The white sarcophagus, the thought that under it was nothing but raw meat, a "skin" without color.

What terrible conflagration of the soul has made me see this way?

Blacks as Threats

Several black boys were on the floor of the gym. As they were leaving, they were approached by a group of white girls. The boys stopped in their tracks. The girls stared back blankly. There was a long moment of hesitation, everyone very conscious. "Y'all hate black people?" one of the boys said, his tone not provocative, just asking for fact, as if that fact were common enough to inquire about as he makes his way across the unsettling floor of the world's heart.

"No," one of the girls replied. Both sides resumed walking. The boys headed right for them, cutting through, a kind of delicious male penetration, and the girls let themselves be broken. The boys moved with exuberance, their faces bright, as if the plague that hangs over their entrances had, for a moment, been lifted.

This reminded me of another story told by black children: A group of middle-class children on a subway, sensing a white woman's fear, had deliberately walked behind her, threateningly close, just to see her reaction. Though they had not spoken, the woman had offered her jewelry and purse—to these middle-class teenagers in school clothes on their way home.

The boy who had told the story said he felt guilty after, grateful he hadn't taken anything, and kind of lost, not knowing why he had done it, as if a part of us were living a life out of our own bodies, a life that flashes like electricity, and leads us to it as if we were zombies.

The Woman from Audubon

Yesterday I did an in-service in Audubon. Afterward, one of the teachers who had spoken most intelligently came over to talk to me. As we were talking, I became aware of the tiny gold Star of David around her neck. This town is white. When I say "white" I mean WHITE. The closest thing they have to something "colored" is the Chinese restaurant. I have the feeling that Jews, too, are rare. *Why would she wear that?* I thought.

For several years I wore my identity like a banner. "Hello, I'm Toi Derricotte, I'm black." My black friends told me to grow up. But I was tired of the pleasant conversation at the bus stop with the person who finally said, "Isn't it terrible? Those colored people are taking over everything!" I didn't want to get close and then be hurt. Better to put the truth out front.

Several years ago, when Bruce and I were looking for an apartment, I answered an ad in an all-white neighborhood. I met the agent (I had learned quickly not to take Bruce because, since he's obviously black, we were never shown what was available, only what they wanted us to see), and we drove to the house together. The lady who lived there, plump and matronly, became friendlier and friendlier as she showed me through the rooms. Finally, we sat down on the sofa and relaxed.

"You're going to love this neighborhood!"

"Will I?"

"Oh yes, you'll fit in perfectly." Before I could imagine what she meant, she went on. "You're Catholic, aren't you?"

I was floored. Nobody had ever guessed my religion before. I felt strangely flattered. Did I have a halo coming out of my head like the Blessed Virgin?

"I *am* Catholic, how did you know?"

"Oh, I'm just good at that sort of thing. . . . What are you anyway? Italian?"

So *that's* where she was heading. I had never had it done this way before—she was a real pro. OK. I can play this game, too. "No," I replied politely.

A pause.

She was waiting for me to volunteer.

"Are you Spanish?"

"No."

Another pause.

"Are you French?"

"No."

Another pause.

How many nationalities could she come up with?

"Are you Portuguese?"

"Syrian?"

"Greek?"

"Lebanese?"

"Armenian?"

"Turkish?"

She began naming sects I had never heard of: "Are you Druse?"

"I'm black." Her face turned red as a hot towel.

"I didn't know blacks were Catholic!" she gasped. I broke out laughing. She couldn't have said anything more likely to defuse me if she had thought about it for weeks.

Suddenly I feel a pang of desire that I should have a cross, a star, some sign of gold to wear so that, before they wonder or ask, I can present a dignified response to the world's interrogations.

Now I remember that the famous artist and naturalist John James Audubon, the man the town must have been named after, was rumored to have been black. The irony! How many of us are out here, without signs, traveling back and forth over the line of sight?

The Lost Children

An excerpt from my mother's book, *Bread on the Waters,* chapter titled "The Lost Children":

> STEAL AWAY, STEAL AWAY,
> STEAL AWAY HOME
> AIN'T GOT LONG TO STAY HERE.
> NEGRO SPIRITUAL

Mama and Papa had four children. Two boys and two girls. Only the girls survived childhood in the bigoted and ignorant society into which they were born.

Naulder was the eldest, then Eleanora, me and Bertram. I was named for Papa's sister; Eleanora was named after her godmother (whom we never knew). I don't know the source of either Naulder's or Bertram's names. Many times I heard that Naulder was the smartest, most beautiful and sweetest of the children. If someone said of me, "Noots surely is a pretty child," someone else invariably countered, "But wait until you see Naulder." If an old aunt praised Eleanora, "You're such a smart girl," another reminded her, "Naulder is much smarter." . . . To the children, Naulder was the general who led us into zones of exploration.

Naulder's light burned intensely—if only for a little while. One summer day, Naulder came running to Mama with some of his playmates. They were singing:

> *Last night, the night before,*
> *twenty-four robbers at my door,*
> *I got up and let them in,*
> *hit 'em on the head with a rollin' pin.*
> *All hid?*

"Mama, Mama, all the kids out playin' hide-and-seek, can I go play too?"

"Where're you going to play, Naulder?"

"Just to the lumber yard, Mama."

There were no playgrounds for Negro children when Naulder lived, no gymnasiums and no swimming pools; they were not allowed to play in the city playgrounds or even public parks. In The Alley there was no space for little boys to romp and run, play jump rope, build their kites and coax them to fly with the wind at their heels. So they left the younger children at home and played at the lumber yard amid the lumber stacks, planks, shavings and nails. . . .

At the lumber yard, the boys joined in the hide-and-seek games, Then it was Naulder's turn to hide.

"No peekin' now," he called, as he scrambled in and out of the stacks of lumber. Then he found a hiding place he liked—back of the tallest stack in the yard.

"All hid?" chanted the children.

Their eyes were closed behind their hands, waiting for his answering call. His familiar "All hid," never rang out. The tallest stack of lumber toppled over. He was crushed to death. . . .

Mama and Papa took Naulder back to her home town, Jeanerette, Louisiana, for burial. Throughout her years, she kept roses blooming beside his tomb, and carried his perfect memory with her like a life-raft, clinging to it to breathe and survive.

I have a misty memory of Naulder. There he is, in his ragged blue short pants, running around the front yard. His black curls flit hither and thither.

Suddenly he stops, glances at me as I sit on the steps playing with my red-haired doll. Then, assured that his little sister is safe, he runs off with his pals to play horseshoes in the dirt.

Throughout many perilous times in my life, I have longed for the protective glance of Naulder.

Bertram, a baby I know little about, didn't survive as long as Naulder. Somehow, the elders never talked about Bertram enough for me to form an image. Did he have curly hair like Mama, or straight hair like Papa? Was his skin white like Papa or olive like Mama? Was he a petulant cry-baby, or a happy, quiet baby? Were the elders so ashamed that he had died such a needless death that they were too remorseful to mention his name?

No old folks' musings long ago, no talk of "Bertram was this," or "Bertram was that," come back to me now. And all I can recall is why and how he died.

In order to go out to work, Mama frequently had to rely on neighbors to stay with her children. It was on one of those days that an old lady who cared for Bertram, scratched the "soft spot" (fontanel) in his skull. He developed an infection and died a few days later. He was not yet three months of age.

Bertram, cheated of life and even of remembrance.

Again Mama made the pilgrimage to Jeanerette, bearing her son's body home. She placed the bodies of her two children together in one tomb in old, picturesque Saint John's cemetery.

Race in the
Creative Writing
Classroom

Baring/Bearing Anger

A few weeks ago I got angry at a student in one of my creative writing classes who complained that I was talking too much about race. She said there were people in the class who were tired of hearing about it. I have heard that complaint from white students before, and in the past, I have been patient, tried to listen and clarify my purposes in a more tolerant manner. This time, however, I found myself tired and lashing out. "If you don't like it, you don't have to stay." She looked devastated. I thought about calling her that night and apologizing, but I didn't. It isn't that I didn't feel sorry for her pain, and it wasn't that I felt completely justified, but I wanted to give us both time to think, and I wanted her to consider the seriousness of what I was trying to do. Sometimes anger can get one's attention.

That night I anguished about my behavior, but I'm sure I didn't feel the vulnerability that my student must have felt. Because of the dynamics of power, I am in a totally different position now in the classroom as a professor than I was as a student.

For many years, not looking black and being the only black student in a traditional graduate English literature department, I never spoke about my race. Partly I didn't speak about it because there didn't seem to be an appropriate time, and partly it was because I felt, never having read a black author all the way through high school, college, and graduate school, that revealing my race might somehow endanger my fragile ambition to be a writer. Once I had asked a professor why we hadn't read any black writers in his class. "We don't go down that low," he had explained. I was too shocked to ask him what he meant. How would his opinion of my papers have changed if I had revealed I was black, or even if I had questioned him about his statement? I thought for a long time about going back to talk to him, but I didn't. It wasn't just that I thought my professors regarded the writings of blacks as inferior, the damage was even more corrosive: I thought that many of them felt black people themselves were incapable, either because of our minds, experiences, or language, of writing "real" literature.

The next day I called my student and we met for coffee. She told me how afraid she had been that she would lose our relationship. She had studied with me for three semesters and I had always been supportive. This was the first time she had seen me angry. I assured her that my anger had passed quickly. But I wanted her to know that, given the history of racism, at least as far as I was concerned, no relationship between blacks and whites will be genuine unless it can bear and bare anger, that bearing and baring anger is the real test of whether a relationship can last.

One of the writing assignments I give new writing students is based on a quote by Red Smith. "There is nothing to writing; all you have to do is sit down and open up a vein." We talk about the pain of revealing ourselves, of getting out what is inside. Later I may ask students to write a letter of unfinished business to someone from their past. Often the first important poems we write, our "breakthrough" poems, are angry. There's something about anger that motivates, that gets us over our "stuckness," over our fear. Often poems seem to burst out whole from some storeroom in the body/mind as if they had been sitting around waiting for years. But there is a danger in anger for black students. White students often write "breakthrough" poems about their childhood. Often called "brave" by the other poets in the class, these poems are frequently painful reassessments of their parents. Black students, however, often don't go back to childhood. They have clear angers that are more weighty right here in the present. There is always a "last straw." Writing about the past is not threatening to others in the class, but writing about what is happening in the classroom here and now is. For the black writer breaking silence, breaking restraint is a frightening step. The person who was the catalyst for the angry poem, unaware of the long history of oppression and internalized rage, takes it as a personal insult. Some students side with the white student, some with the black, but most students remain silent, afraid to go in either direction. In any event, the black student may lose a few of his or her best supporters, people who can tolerate poems about race as long as they don't make anybody feel too uncomfortable. I have had people give me "gifts" after reading a poem of mine, quotations from the Bible or other calming and inspirational words suggesting ways to find love and inner peace. As Cornelius Eady says, presenting reference to students' work. More important, providing information may remove the burden on black students to be the primary sources of information about blackness and let them get on with their own work. For its facts, figures, and readability, I suggest Andrew Hacker's *Two Nations: Black and White, Separate, Hostile, Unequal.* A provocative video about images of blacks in the media, *Ethnic Notions,* should stimulate useful dialogue. Of course, teachers should include writers of color in their lists of required reading.

Hayes Davis, a student in my senior seminar, wrote this poem in response to a white student's complaints.

BLACK WRITERS

> I don't really give a rat's ass
> if you're tired of reading black poets,
> but I do, really, and I couldn't help
> but think, if I want to write
> for this class any more, I have to
> start editing myself a little now
> and I'm angry about that
> and I'm not going to let
> you edit me through myself,
> or are you really tired of me?
> Are you tired of me, or Huie, or Cassandra,
> are you tired of Toi?
> Why the fuck are you in the class,
> or are we acceptable black poets,
> or were you thinking there wouldn't
> be any black poets in the class?
> Are we not really black poets?
> Poets that happen to be black
> ya know, but not really like black, ya know?

Race is a scary subject. Discussions about it in a diverse community are fraught with dangers. People walk on eggs. My husband uses flip charts when he makes presentations in the corporate world. Being the only black person in the room most of the time, he feels people hear him better when they aren't looking at his face. But we as writers are told to reveal ourselves.

Michele Elliot wrote very sparingly during her two years as a graduate student, and what she wrote she was careful about sharing. Though she had shared little in class, she had made many comments to me about her discomfort as one of two black students in the class, of her sadness that classmates—even people she respected and liked—lacked understanding of the most basic aspects of racism and made comments about her poems that completely missed the boat. Finally, something triggered the release of many years of anger.

> Perhaps you will never be able to experience these lines, perhaps you will dismiss me as absurd, inflexible, acting difficult as an unruly child. Maybe you will never feel the colonization of your own mind, notice the weight of its chains. You're defensive and you don't even realize it. You're asking me questions you've already created the answers for, formed hypotheses, collected data and published the results. What would happen if the world split open and you were forced to face the scared, uncomfortable you, the unlistened to, unrecognizable you, unable to put your feet down, orient yourself. The rules are gone, no walls to hide behind, left on the plantation without a gun. You can't shut it down, package it, contain it. It's exploding everywhere. The gaps are too big to bridge. In it you can hear the violence of your own words, see the consequences. Language has left you alone, lonely. You're without an agenda, a place to be. Everything is at stake, raw and unbearable.

For Ms. Eliot the most violent and revengeful fantasy she could imagine was for the tables to be turned, for the one who has privilege to walk the line between worlds, to see with double vision from the eyes of the "other." A white woman in one of my classes, Kristen Herbert, wrote a collection of poems titled *White Space* in which she interrupted the normal lines of the poem with cutouts, so that you could open up the flaps and read what was underneath, what was inside the white space. Whiteness has to be examined, addressed, not taken as "normal." White people have to develop a double consciousness, too, a part in which they see themselves as "other." We are all wounded by racism, but for some of us those wounds are anesthetized. When we begin to feel it, we're awake.

I want to talk about anger, about how important it is as a part of the process of coming to one's voice, about how it is inevitable in a diverse classroom. I want to talk about how powerful it is, how dangerous it is, how mysterious, about how suddenly real feelings start to emerge. If we don't recognize anger, if we don't allow for it, if we're not ready, if we don't, in fact, welcome it as a creative force, then I think we're going to end up blaming and dividing people even more. We hesitate to allow it to happen, though anger is a part of life. (So often "life" is not allowed in the classroom.)

At the same time that we move toward clarity about our differences, it is also possible to move toward clarity about what makes us human, the same. The edges of the workshop are ragged. But I have seen a few black and white students bare and bear their own raw truths.

Grad Class

Last week, at a panel on teaching creative writing in a diverse classroom, I read an essay I had written about an incident that had happened several years ago in a graduate class I was teaching.

Some of the white students in my class are very angry. They feel that they are being attacked, not listened to, silenced. It hurts. It makes them angry. And they don't know what to do.

Some of the black students in my class are very angry. They feel that they have been attacked, not listened to, silenced. It hurts. It makes them angry. They have tried for years to be silent. But finally it is coming out.

Some of the gays, some of the straights, some of the men, some of the women, some of everybody is walking on a tightrope, and I am the teacher. What am I responsible for? For "educating" them to new material? For allowing them to speak? For encouraging them to dig deeper? For saying "put it all in your work?" For being quiet? For talking? For telling my own personal truth?

Everything one says can be misunderstood, used against one, piled up as evidence, used to support something one did not intend. Everything one does not say can cause a vacuum in which much destructive force can appear.

I saw it happen once, in a course I was teaching. During the semester a black man began flirting with a white woman. You could see he was very attracted, and the woman seemed not to be attracted, but something slightly more. She was conversational when he approached, but at the same time pulled away. There was a kinetic energy between them that seemed to be based on something more than their personal likes and dislikes. He was affronted. He was a beautiful, strong-looking man who, I sensed, was not accustomed to rejection. This was his first semester away from home, one black man in a group of strangers, and in the school he had come from, a black school, he had been a powerful and known entity. I sensed his pain at real-izing that what our society had, on the one hand, taught him was most useful about himself—his body—was at the same time powerless to get what he had been taught was the most desirable thing—a beautiful blonde. He could only get so far. And he wasn't willing to accept that.

She, on the other hand, I couldn't figure out. I resented her because he seemed to want her. A white woman. A beautiful blonde. I felt jealous for the black girls who weren't wanted. I felt jealous for myself, who I feel had never been able to attract such a beautiful black man. Maybe I wanted him. Or wished I had been so wanted by some black man. My father? Or was it my own desire and inability to touch that so confused me?

I could feel him aggressively positioning himself and she defensively responding. There seemed to develop an unspoken wall between them, and they both began doing things that seemed to mean the opposite of what was apparent, so that when she smiled, it seemed she most wanted to get away, and when he pursued her, it was as if he was really ignoring her, ignoring her block.

His male assertiveness seemed to change into aggression, and her self-containment into patroniza-tion. It frightened me. I've known men and women enter into mortal combat like that, with terrible reper-cussions for everyone in their path. I wanted to stop the escalation. I especially feared the man's anger. My father was an angry man. When I challenged him, I feared for my life. And I did challenge him. But often, at the thought of confronting an escalating anger, I bowed to it, rolled over and played dead. This woman wasn't playing dead. She was more determined. And he was more in her face. I feared for him, too. And for me. I felt called forth to take a side, to be loyal. Just as much as I resented what I perceived to be her arrogance, I was equally afraid of what I perceived to be his assertion of entitlement. In a way, I wanted him to fight. But no. How could I want him to fight for something so wrong to fight for? A white woman? A blonde? And what about the right of any woman for any reason to say no?

Once they were standing together, and I felt something so alive between them. I wanted them to go to bed with each other, to make love, for all of us. I wanted them to be the most beautiful couple at the ball, for black assertion to win and white resistance to give in, for male desire to change the frightened heart that wanted to shield itself. There was something that I wanted to stop, yet it was like watching an oncoming collision, hoping that, at the last moment, what looked like a dangerous confrontation would somehow turn, not into an unbreachable distance or a deadly fight, but into the joining of whatever we have been trained to keep apart by instinct.

It didn't happen that way. At that very moment when I was hoping, she raised her hand, feeling or patting or petting his hair. He felt that moment as an invasion—how dare she touch his head?—and it brought up the nearly instinctual rage at the "good-luck" rub—white people who had said for generations that you can get good luck by rubbing a black boy's head. Why had she touched his head? We never found out. But, saying he had felt "raped" by that touch, he wrote an enraged poem in which he raped a woman. Which engendered her saying that his poem was a public humiliation to her and screaming that she had been raped in actuality when she was young and nobody could do this to her in a poem.

People were moved and sorry for her, and he was soon isolated, except for the few blacks in the class.

Some people claimed, on his behalf, that a rape in a poem is not the same as a rape in life. And he said the person raped in the poem was not her. But he didn't back down from his isolation and rage, and he didn't say he was sorry.

Who was wrong? Who right? Most of us tried to settle the confrontation by taking sides. In a way, I think both of them were reacting to something much larger, and neither had the wisdom to make us comfortable by saying so. It made us all, poor poets who probably have receded into poetry precisely because we want nothing to do with such out-and-out confrontation, show our worst side.

The day after I read this, I got a call. Editors from a major magazine wanted to publish it. I am afraid. Will I make people I love angry and hate me for revealing their "dark" secrets? Do I have the right? Is this a "true" story? Or just my sick need to see always, as my mother said, "the bad"?

I had decided to publish and be damned, because "the truth" has to be told by somebody: Racism isn't out there, it's in here, within our families and the community we most love and want to love us. How can we tell the truth about the people we love without hurting them and breaking our needed connection? How can we do it without accomplishing a terrible thing—putting in the place of that unrealized hope for connection, that continuous and painful longing, this "necessity," which feels cold and hard, violent, this withdrawal, a choice that puts in my soul a danger— emptiness, loneliness, a stuckness behind an untranslatable puzzle, a cold spot, a detachment that I "bear" with dignity because I am to "blame," either unconsciously, because of my human flaws, or because I have chosen the "brave" route.

The choice feels so lonely that I want to die, tell whatever truth and then die, perhaps kill myself rather than live with that hopeless sense of violence to those I love, and that pain so impossible to bear, that they will never trust me, that I can never trust myself, and that I cannot say I'm sorry, because, as my father said, it's too late. Sorry never helps.

My father chose coldly like that. He said he'd never apologize; he said you mustn't be weak, never say you're sorry. What he did he did. Perhaps, locked in his house, unable to get out because of his leg, in his seventies, having, in his youth, driven away his mother, driven away my mother, and his second wife, he sat alone in that upstairs window with his police radio and his speakers turned up, which were connected to the outside so he could hear his neighbors' goings and comings—the sound of crackling paper as they lifted grocery sacks—perhaps he felt that painful inability to connect.

A woman I recently met spent the night with me. This morning she said, "I want to talk to you about that story you wrote. I see it's important to you. That story is really about you and me, it's about how we are attracted to each other and yet you pull away." And she said, wisely, "What you must do is show how that story is really about you, about your story, about your struggle and need to heal. That's what you haven't shown, and it puts an entirely different light on the story."

I said, "Then it makes it personal, and I don't want it to be merely personal."

And she said, "Oh no. It's much more than about gender or race, it's about being human, and even more than being human, it's about being human at the end of the twentieth century. That's what you have to put back in."

For so long I struggled to eviscerate the personal. I thought I was following Eliot's dictum to let the metaphor speak. I thought I was proving, like the victim at a trial who sticks to the facts, that my "story" is "real."

What I realize is that I am always mixing up the world with my own soul, so that when I see these two people coming close and moving away, really, it is not about the world at all—or, as my friend said, it *is* about the world, about the human condition, but the metaphor is not something that one finds in the world. Eliot was wrong. The metaphor is in *me*, and not acknowledging the self, pretending there is no self, or only a thread of self, one portrays falsely. One does not see the metaphor out there as if one were focusing on a movie, the only way into understanding is to put *in* the self, the most "juicy" part.

Four months ago, in January, I went out with a man in his sixties. I have lived apart from my husband for eight years, and this was my first "date." We held hands and, that night, after a year and a half of seeing him at public places and having sporadic conversations with him on the phone, I let him kiss and touch me on the inside. It was the first time in twenty-seven years that I have let anyone touch me like that except my husband. Why did you do it? my new friend asked. And I said because I wanted to see if I would die, if I would go crazy. I started weeping as I told her, because I had felt nothing. I had felt detached, but I was glad I had done it, glad to see that I wouldn't die.

I had hung a Peruvian rug over the window. I suppose I hadn't wanted anyone to see inside. He didn't stay overnight, but I left the rug up, and the next morning, when the sun shone through its dark patterns, it looked as if streaks of wet, bloody skin were hanging at the window, as if the light were shining through raw skin.

Fearful desire. Dangerous longing.

How can I publish these words when they come so much out of my own sickness? Without answers, do I cause more harm? Shams threw Rumi's book down a well and said, "If you want, I can pull it up with every sheet dry, or you can follow me." I want to burn the book until the sickness dies in *me*.

Before I had read the piece, I had thought about how it "spills the beans" on people I long not to hurt, offend, people I love. I looked out over the audience and tried to decide what to do. I realized my fearful tendency to do something impulsive and regret it. I had brought something "safe" to read. And yet, as often happens, the "safe" piece just didn't seem right.

I saw the face of a woman I love, Alicia Ostriker, a great poet and lover of poets, a white woman who I know would have wanted me to read that work. I knew she was one who, even if I had pointed out to her something she had done that hurt me, wouldn't have abandoned our friendship.

I looked around the room again. There were people in the room who knew the people I had written about. I knew my story would get back and that, though the point of the story was totally the opposite, people would take sides, find reasons to bolster their own points of view.

Then, in the middle of my shaky fear, I remembered my present graduate class, who had come to the reading. There was a whole row of them, the second row, so close to me. I could sense them through my downturned eyes, sitting with a kind of exactness and tension in their bodies, a readiness to receive. I felt an opening of my heart that happens, like everything of wonder always does, in a great wave of surprise—love coming in the middle of my fear. And that inspired me to feel my place in my work, my home. I read what I read because of those I love and who love me, and somehow, that is a part of my braveness.

Later, at dinner, the white woman sitting across from me told me how much she was moved by what I had read. She said that several people had remarked that the story made them cry. She talked about the part where the young black man and white woman had come together, how I wished that they could make love for all of us. She told me about her own blond daughter and the young black man whom she kissed and nuzzled in the backyard of the house that had opened onto the world. The relationship didn't last, and now she has a beautiful, dark grandchild, an eight-year-old who said to her last week, "Gramma, I wish I was white."

She told me how inadequate she felt when her grandchild had said that. What could she, a white woman, know of her grandchild's feelings? What could she say? She kept saying to her grandchild, "Why do you wish that? You're beautiful just as you are. You're beautiful." But she looked at me as if she was accusing herself of what mothers always accuse themselves of, of never getting it right.

I told her how important it was that her grandchild could speak to her, how, sometimes, I couldn't go to black women, how sometimes, no, not sometimes, but for many, many years, it was white women whom I poured my soul out to, white women I wasn't afraid would hate me or leave, it was white women, maybe precisely because they didn't have the same agony about race, who could still trust me, listen. Perhaps their generosity was based on naïveté, ignorance, on their own prejudice—wouldn't it be nice to have one black friend to take under one's wing? Whatever the motive, my need made myself available to it.

I have laid my soul bare to Mady, to Camille, to Marilyn, to Sarah, to Alicia, to Sharon, to Mary Jane, to Nancy, to so many strangers I have met at workshops, so many women like this woman sitting across the table, I have trusted as I didn't trust my family, my oldest friends. Maybe, somewhere in all that, love comes in a mysterious way, the way I came upon the faces of my students at the reading and suddenly knew I loved them.

What has happened between black people is sometimes so intense that a certain kind of sharing is too frightening. All those years when I had to say the most horrible thing—that, yes, I felt deep conflicts about who I am and who I want to be, that I often felt a shock of distance when I saw a person on the street with dark skin—it was white women I could say this to. I was afraid to say these things to the ones whose love and understanding I most longed for.

At that moment I thanked all the white women who have listened, who have befriended me, who have made a net over which I walked somewhat safely, the ones who were there for me to speak my self-doubt to, my justified angers, the ones willing to meet me more than halfway. I told her not to worry, that she was a great blessing to her granddaughter, whose longings and fears make clear the deepest shadows of the heart.

We shared pictures of our grandchildren, and she

pointed out how ironic it is that I have a blond grandchild, a child who could be white, whereas she has a dark grandchild. A black woman sitting across from a white woman talking about race, while the most significant and dramatic thing is happening out of our conscious control—our genetic selves are changing, the white woman's self turning darker and the black woman's self turning whiter.

Perhaps "race" isn't something that locks us into separate groups. Perhaps it is a state that floats back and forth between us, equally solid and unreal, as if our body and soul were kept apart and, like a kind of Siamese twins, joined only by the thin cord of desire.

Diaries at an Artists Colony

Arriving for a stay of a few weeks, I was happy to find another black artist—who, unfortunately, was leaving on the day after I arrived. Coincidence? Or were we "tokens"? That question colored the rest of my time there. And another black artist arrived on the day I was leaving.

Black Arms

A group of us are sitting around the TV room. Bill, a painter from the South, is talking about how hard his mother works. He says, "I told her all you need is a pair of good black arms." The others snicker.

I am new here. All I want to do is get along. I say nothing, though now I know there is a part of me that is a joke to this man—my washerwoman great-grandmother, my cook grandmother.

I will be silent. I want him to like me. I want to tell him how he hurts. But then the colonists will say, "You know how sensitive they are." I will be labeled. For six weeks, the only black person, I will never sit at the table without "Black Arms."

Dinnertime

Last night at the dinner table, John, a man who didn't know I'm black, noticed the book of women's diary writing that has a section of *The Black Notebooks* in it.

He asked to see the book, and when he took it I

could see he wasn't going to skim over the table of contents. He went directly for my story, putting down his fork, and began to read. I felt a coldness, like a breeze ruffling a curtain on a line. The other dinner tables were quiet; many of the colonists don't know I'm black. I could just hear him blurt out, "I didn't know you're black. You don't look black. How did you get that color?"

I don't like to lose control that way. I fear being questioned or attacked, like an animal in a cage, prodded and poked by onlookers.

The man, fortunately, limited his comments to the quality of the work. "This is great. It sent a shiver up my spine. It's dramatic."

The other people at the table didn't know the content. Not that I mind every person at the colony knowing I'm black. I don't care, and I am proud of my work. But when several come at me from all sides, I don't know which way to turn. And heaven help me if I should show anger or be defensive.

John wouldn't let it alone. Later, when several of us were sitting around the fireplace, he said, "You should read this article in the *Times*. You'll like it. It reminds me of your book." I hadn't seen the article, but I knew it must be about black people. As soon as he knew I was black, I became a category, and now anything he reads by or about a black person reminds him of me.

A Chinese man who has also read my book said, "This article is nothing like the writing in Toi's book." I was glad he spoke, defending the uniqueness of my experience.

Later, John was playing pool. I was sitting twenty feet away and noticed him staring at me. I thought he was thinking I was attractive and was beginning to feel flattered. Suddenly he yelled across the room. "You really should read that article. You'll find it interesting, really timely."

"What's it about?" another man called out.

"Racism," he yelled back.

The people in the room looked up. I felt the conversation go out of my hands.

The other man said, "That isn't timely. It's ongoing and eternal."

I was glad somebody spoke. And it wasn't me.

The Testimony of Innocence

Last night I went over to Emily's studio to share my work. She read my diary entries and I read her poems. She said my diary entries were extremely important. She asked whom they were addressed to, and I read her the entry that described my audience: " . . . all the people in my past, black and white, who represent the internalized process of racism within me."

When I began writing *The Black Notebooks*, I wrote mainly for myself, although at the back of my mind was an idea that maybe I would find the courage to make it public. I wanted to tell the truth, however painful, but also to write for the larger human community—the world. I know that sounds ridiculously grandiose, but I felt an honest confession would have merit. My negative self-concept made me trust myself more than writers whose descriptions of racism are testimonies of their own innocence. I have always distrusted that, both from whites and blacks.

My skin color causes certain problems continuously, problems that open the issue of racism over and over like a wound. These openings are occasions for reexamination. My skin keeps things, literally, from being either black or white.

I know where I would like this all to end. I would like to be done with shame, to know I love myself and my own people, to believe that I have something positive to offer, that I am not unlovable, not because I am black, but because I am weak of character and disloyal, because there is something intrinsically wrong with me. I want it to end with some answer, some illumination that makes me see myself and the world in a new way. Then I will put the triumphant closing chapter on the diary and publish it, with pity, even disdain, for that woman who had written it.

I'll publish. I'll make a name for myself. I'll make money. I'll win the love of my relatives and get a full professorship at a university. I'll win a movie contract and play the heroine of my own story. It seems awful to hope that success will come from this.

Not to worry, my friend Cherrie says, writing about racism doesn't make you successful, it makes you ignored.

Coming Out

I still have not said anything to the painter from the South, though last night he said something about running off with a Puerto Rican woman. I am afraid to come out as a black person, to bear that solitude, that hatred, that invisibility. But I am also holding back something, a gift. I don't want to be a rejected gift, a piece of shit. Yet I can't expect love. I give myself because giving is right, because I make myself strong.

Bill

After breakfast I saw him lumbering toward his Jeep. He looked a little lost; several of his close friends have left. I had heard him say another gem this morning: "I wish I had ten little black women to sew the holes in that canvas. . . ."

Every time the opportunity comes to talk to him, the time doesn't seem right. Either other people are around or there's another problem. After his art show last night, I stayed longer than anyone, but he seemed depressed by people's reactions. It would have been piling shit on top of shit if I had tried to talk to him; and I don't think he would have heard what I was saying. I found myself listening to his worries, reassuring him, and kicking myself for being a coward.

But this morning was perfect. I know he often goes into town for donuts. I had been on my way to my studio, but I turned in my tracks.

Sitting in the donut shop, the comforting cups of coffee were placed before us. He lit a cigarette. "There's something I have to tell you," I said. "I'm black, and last week when you made that comment about black arms, it made me feel bad. And this morning you said something about little black women sewing up holes in canvas." I didn't say it in a mean voice, just a human voice, one on one. (Inside, I'm saying, *Why can't I just blurt it out? Why do I have to be so careful?*)

I tried not to look at his face so I could get my words out, but I caught a glimpse and saw a muscle twitching in his cheek; his mouth was slightly open, and he was listening intently. I went on, "You see, I wanted to say something when this happened last week, but I didn't want to say something that would make people look at me as if I'm different. Sometimes when people find out I'm black, they treat me differently. So when people say things that hurt, I don't know what to do. I want to tell them. But at the same time, I'm afraid I'll be hurt even more."

He started to explain, "When I said that about 'black

arms,' I was repeating something my mother-in-law said, and I was repeating it because I was horrified. What you feel must be similar to what I feel at my wife's house, because I am the only goy." I was happy he was identifying, but I hate it when, after I let a white person know they've said something racist, I end up having to listen for hours to the story of their life. "Please, I don't want to put you on the spot. I just want you to understand my feelings. Do you understand? What do you hear me saying?" He said, "I hear you saying that certain comments which other people make without sensitivity have great poignancy to you because you are black." That wasn't exactly what I was saying, but it seemed close. Besides, it had taken all the bravery I could muster to come this far, I couldn't press him further.

In the past, I have left conversations like this empty, not getting what I wanted. I thought it was rage I wanted to vent. But today, because he listened, because I waited for the right moment and asked for what I wanted, I thought, maybe I've found the answer. From now on, if I just wait, talk about my feelings honestly, if I don't expect the person to say something to take my pain away, if I just ask him or her to repeat back what I've said until they've understood, then everything will be fine.

I want so much to find a formula! Of course, there is none. Sometimes it will come out OK, and sometimes I will walk away with a hole in my heart which all the black women in the world cannot sew up.

Saturday Night

Several colonists sat around trying to have fun on a Saturday night. We miss New York, movies, Chinese restaurants. We talked about feminism, about how, these days, many of the young girls have babies while in high school.

A Southern lady said, "That's what black girls have been doing for years. They have babies and their families raise them. Maybe it's catching up with white girls."

This is the same woman who three days ago was talking about how black people have "funny" names. "They name their kids the strangest things." I thought about the twins in New Jersey whose mother had honored the doctor who had delivered them by giving them the names he had suggested: Syphily and Gonorra.

This woman loves to talk about black people. She's our resident expert. She said, "There aren't any black people here. I haven't seen any."

"Yes there are," I said, smiling.

"Who?"

"You're looking at one."

"You're not really black. Just an eighth or something."

"I don't know how black I am, but I am black."

"Was your mother black?"

"My mother, my father, my grandparents. They are black, and they look just like me."

"How do you know you're black?"

"I'm black because the first people I touched and loved were black."

A woman at the table said, "Did you read the article in *The New York Times* that said if they were strict about genetics, sixty percent of the people in the United States would be classified as black?"

I looked around the table; I was laughing. The others were not. They were worried about how black I was and they should have been worrying about how black *they* were.

I thought of all the little white children, the light of their mothers' and fathers' eyes, in Montana, in flat Wyoming, in Idaho, in lakey Michigan; I thought of that "funny" blackness inside of them, a kernel in each little heart put there, somehow, in the night, like a visit from the tooth fairy. Somewhere babies are popping out of women and no one understands where they come from.

I smile at that heart of darkness in sixty out of a hundred babies, the drop of blood that can't lie to statistics, that will be bled out, measured, and put in a crystal tube. That blood gives those little ones a special light. Wherever I look I see brothers, sisters, who want to break out of their cramped skins, singing with love.

That

Emily said yesterday she was surprised that Pat had called the colony a "white establishment," and said she was uncomfortable with some of the people. Emily hadn't noticed any of "that." Had I noticed any of "that"?

I was on guard. So many times if a black person admits discomfort, the white person then says that the black person must be "sensitive—paranoid"—responding not to the present environment, which is safe and friendly, but to something in the past. They want to hear that the white people in this environment (themselves) are fine. It's the black person who is crazy.

I said, "It's not something that is done consciously; but most of the white people here have had limited exposure to blacks; there are bound to be great problems in communication. There are some people who hate and fear blacks and don't want to be under the same roof. For example, Jan told me Sandra said, when she saw no black people in the dining room, 'Good. I'm glad there are no black people. After New York, this is refreshing.' "

Emily said sometimes when she is with black people, she doesn't know what to do; no matter what she does, it seems to be the wrong thing. She had invited a black woman, a lawyer, over to her house for dinner, and during the dinner conversation the guests at the table started talking about Arabs raising the price of everything in England. Emily said she didn't think they were saying anything racist, and even if they were, what did the Arabs have to do with this black woman? But the woman stood up from the table and said, "I'm sorry, I find this conversation extremely embarrassing." Emily asked me, did I think the woman was right?

I told her, "Emily, frequently white people who have been made uncomfortable by something a black person says or does go to another black person to try to ease the pain, to feel vindicated. First of all, I wasn't there, I don't know what she responded to. Secondly, there would be no way to find out unless both of you could sit down and talk to each other."

Emily said, "That will never happen because she has never asked me out, and when I called her she was cold."

"Black people don't like pain either."

There are so few friendships between whites and blacks in which the people are really themselves. Even when white people try, they are often operating on stereotypes, and though the black person might want to accept them, the only way to break the stereotypes is to tell the truth, which causes pain. A black person and a white person are not just two individuals who have to decide whether they like each other, but representatives carrying huge expectations, beliefs that they must scale like dangerous mountains trying to reach each other.

Gale's Studio

I visited Gale yesterday. I went there feeling greatly honored that she had asked me, since artists prize their time alone and don't want to be disturbed. I had just come into her room, sat down on the mattress, and received a cup of tea when she took off Mozart and asked me if I wanted to hear one of her favorite records, a record about the New York prison Attica. The hair on the back of my neck stood up. What connection had she made between me and Attica?

Give her a chance, I thought, calming myself, maybe it's just a coincidence.

It was atrocious. A white band had taken the departing words of a prisoner and repeated them over and over, as if to make certain that we caught the significance. Atonal music in the background, everything got louder and crashed to an end.

I sat there embarrassed, feeling the need to receive her gift with enthusiasm. She waited. The only word that came to my mind was "interesting."

She started flipping through her collection of classical music to find something else especially for me. "I have a record of Paul Robeson. Would you like to hear that?" *Oh God, it wasn't a coincidence!*

"No, thank you."

She seemed puzzled and at a loss. Finally, she asked, "There is a picture around here of a black man I liked. I slept with him. Would you like to see that?"

I gaped at her innocent face: Gale, the woman I head for at dinnertime because she is not pompous or intimidating, one of the only people I feel comfortable with.

I told her that just because I am black doesn't mean I am one-dimensional. I told her that I am interested in many things. I like classical music and know quite a bit about it. She said, "But my other black friends like it when I play those records." She looked genuinely hurt.

I told her all black people are different. She said, "But I've tried so hard. I'm tired of always trying to please them." She looked at me in anger. I was one more proof of her inadequacy, as if I should have taken whatever was offered and let her feel generous and good.

I left abruptly, sorry for my anger, sorry for what I had learned about her, sorry that she had lost her feeling of closeness, however illusory, to black people—sorry, sorry, sorry—and somehow to blame. I had felt close to her; now I distrusted my instincts and dreaded an isolation deeper than any I had experienced before.

Jazz

Now that I am the "known" black, everything with a tinge of blackness on it is delivered to me.

Mark, the composer, who has been talking about Mozart at the dinner table for days, comes running up to me this afternoon when he sees me on the path, his face lit like a beacon. He doesn't even bother with a greeting.

"Guess what I've been doing today?" he blurts.

I can't imagine.

"I've been writing JAZZ," he presents, as if it were a Cartier jewel on a silver platter.

What am I supposed to say? You must be a really nice white guy? Thanks for taking us seriously?

"Good for you," I answer, and walk on as quickly as possible.

Crazy Thoughts

How beautiful the view from my desk of wild-flowers through the cathedral-tall window. I watch the lovely black birds. How kind the lunch on my door-step, the vegetable torte with white cream sauce, the chocolate cake. How pleasing the flower on the table, the yellow Victorian sofa, the barn of colorful chickens. Kind and specific the words in the office, the locks on my doors. I am treated like a queen. But when the lights go off, I face my fears.

Why is my stomach in knots? Why do I fear that during the night I'll be smothered? I think poison gas will come out of the register. I think the people are monsters, not artists, and that during the night they will implant a small radio in my brain. How can I think this? The memory of my father being smoth-ered by a pillow my grandmother put over his head when he was three? In the morning I am ashamed.

I try desperately to make friends, hoping I will actu-ally feel that trust that makes the knots in my stom-ach loosen. I was terrified to come here; I always feel frightened, except when I'm near home. I trust no one—especially not myself.

I try to do my work. This is a perfect environment. No cleaning. No cooking. I needn't even go to get lunch; it is placed in a basket outside my door by a man on tiptoes. Wood is stacked. I make a fire. I sit in the sun. I want to be grateful. I am grateful. But the sickness backs up in my throat like phlegm.

In the kitchen the cook speaks softly. I want to sit by her all day and stay away from the roads on which I have been hurt by a word. But she is cooking and I don't want to bother her. Please, let me not bother anyone. Let me leave the tub without a hair. Let me not speak to those who turn their bodies slightly away. I must notice this.

No one can help. Only I, myself. But how can I let go? My face is a mask, like Uncle Tom's, my heart twisted with rage and fear.

After

After I came back I was sick for several weeks. I felt completely wrung out, run-down. I had left smiling, beaming, thanking everyone—the kitchen help, the office help, the yard help—for their kindness. My friend came to pick me up. The night before we were to drive home, I sat with her in the restaurant—the first black face I had seen in weeks—and for an instant, I felt my body falling under me, as if I had slipped under the wheels of a train. I had made it until the last minute, keeping a stiff upper lip, and here I was, so close to the end, finally about to lose it.

They were so sorry to see me go they offered me a stay of two more weeks. If I stayed, I would be proving my desperate bravery to myself. But I declined. I was tired of feeling frightened and wanted to go home, where I felt safe.

A Jewish activist friend returned shortly after and asked me to please write a letter telling them how hard it had been to be the only black person there. She had found the same token during her stay. I postponed it and postponed it. I didn't want to. I had been a success—I had gone someplace far from home and stayed four weeks without having a nervous breakdown. And they had tried to do everything to please me—cooked for me, cleaned up after me, put wood in my fireplace. I didn't have the heart to tell them I had been miserable and frightened the whole time. Besides, I wanted to be a "successful" black, a person they would ask back, a person who would ease the way for others. "See, we're not as bad as you thought."

The day my friend returned from the colony, she was full of news about how she had written a letter to the board, sent the names and addresses of black artists. The president had talked to her for a half hour about how pleased he was with her efforts. The next day she called me, despondent. Her editor had called from her large publishing house—they were remaindering her book. I felt so sorry for her. I told my husband about her efforts and how she had come home to this big disappointment. "I'm not surprised," he said. "Somebody from the colony must have gotten to somebody at her publishing house and they iced her." I looked at my husband angrily. "Oh, that's silly," I said. "One has nothing to do with the other." But I felt the ground under me sinking.

Face
to Face

Now we see indistinctly, as in a mirror,
then we will see face to face.

I Corinthians 13:12

The Drugstore

When we moved to Upper Montclair, there were almost no black people who frequented the stores. When I went into the drugstore, I wondered if word had spread, if the pharmacist and clerks knew I was a member of the black family that had moved in—or if I was invisible, if they thought I was just another housewife. I didn't want to be treated "differently," if they treated me differently it meant they thought I was less, inferior. I felt my way through months, alert, like a worm taken out of the dirt, my head lifted, sniffing the air with my whole being.

I was afraid to ask for credit, even though the other women asked for a charge on their first visit; I was terrified to be rejected. I didn't say much; my personality wasn't exactly like theirs. I laughed at slightly different things. I thought they would be able to sense my fear.

One day, after I had spent several hundred dollars in the store, I asked for credit. The clerk didn't blink an eye. Maybe she doesn't know, I thought. Slowly, I began to bring my self into the store—my friendliness, my neighborly questions, "How is your wife doing?" I asked for advice: "Can you suggest a cold pill?" All the time I was charging, paying my bill on time, building bridges I walked on tentatively, holding my hat, watching for the escape route.

Months went by. I brought my jokes into the store, kidded the pharmacist. He laughed. Would he go over the line and say something belittling? I loosened up. We had worked out a way to speak to each other—not like with the manager of the fruit store, who found out I was black and started flirting, pinching my arm.

Toni Snead moved to Upper Montclair. She is dark, married to a doctor. We became friends because she was having many of the same self-doubts I was having. We talked together several times a week. We helped each other through hard times. We both saw a therapist.

I could go to her house when I had no place else to go, stop in her kitchen for a cup of coffee, and sit with the dishes undone. She could see me in my torn bathrobe and dirty house shoes. There was so much we laughed about—like the time the couple from across the street came for dinner (I was showing off my newly remodeled kitchen) and, just as the doorbell rang, I stepped with my long gown into the deluxe Jenn-air frying pan full of grease which I had put, for a moment, on the floor. I had to go to the door dragging my soaked skirt, leaving a trail of slime like a mummy. I invited them into the kitchen and, as I mopped up the congealing grease and they sat with vodka and limes, large drops of water started to plunk down on their heads. We looked up—there was a leak through the light fixture from upstairs, where my husband had taken a shower.

We took delight in stories like that. We sat in our kitchens and howled, tears streaming down our faces. We were so glad to have found each other. I loved her because I felt so comfortable loving her, so unafraid that I would say the wrong thing. I knew no matter how much I hurt, she wouldn't hurt me more because of it.

Months went by. She was the only one who mattered. Let the others sink into the earth, let them be swept underground by earthquakes—every white house, neat lawn, every station wagon full of clean children, every cherry tree and rhododendron. Let them all go to hell. She was the only one who mattered.

One day I was in the drugstore, shopping without thinking. I walked down the aisle like a known customer. I had a smile on my face. I felt someone touch my shoulder and, when I turned, it was Toni. When I saw her dark face, inside, I felt my arms, which were reaching for her, pull away. My heart shrank, and everything came back—the months, the years, the fear of being recognized. As if I hated her! As if she were not the only living being in the world. I greeted her warmly but my heart was a cold thing that could have been plucked out of my chest and eaten.

Years passed.

I told a white woman, a friend, what I had done. "Terrible," she said. "Terrible to deny someone in your heart you love." And she looked at me as if I were not human.

Years passed.

I told Toni—how I had hated to see her standing before me. How I had wanted her to disappear. She said she had known nothing of this when I touched her. I told her how I hated myself.

Journal entry:

This week I sent Toni the journal entry about the drugstore. Even though I had told her the story last year and she had forgiven me, I was still afraid of her reaction when she saw my feelings in writing.

I called her and, when she picked up the phone, said, "Just tell me you don't hate me. I don't care if you're angry. Just say you don't hate me."

She said she was surprised by the depth of feelings in the story, but that even though she had come home tired, it hadn't disturbed her.

She said the one thing that had bothered her is that I had called her dark. She said, "After all these years of looking in the mirror, I should know I'm dark."

Revealing I'm Black

I still have that response when I see a dark person, not just a black person, in some nearly all-white environment—the feelings of distance and recognition, a knotting internally as if I were trying to push something away, a narrowing of my vision, or rather my preoccupation. Perhaps this only occurs in situations in which *I* feel isolated and vulnerable, for this doesn't happen in places where there are many black people present and where I feel that my blackness—or perhaps not even my blackness, but my "difference"—would be accepted. In a grocery store in which there are a lot of people of color, for example, or on a bus, I feel as if there is a little community established. Perhaps I perceive others differently because I perceive myself differently. I get into conversations with other black people which are so friendly it makes me think they know I'm black, or else black people are totally more friendly than white people, or perhaps *I* am friendlier to black people than to white and, therefore, they are friendlier back.

Revealing I'm black, even to black people, can cause a moment of discomfort. So that twenty minutes into the conversation, often they say something that lets me know they didn't "get" it. Perhaps there is a kind of cautiousness, a period of checking me out. Am I some crazy white lady professing to be black for God knows what reason? Black people, too, may resist having their minds yanked around. On my first meeting with a principal in an all-black school, I told him a story about not being recognized as black. "Is that your way of letting me know you're a sister?" he asked cannily.

I suppose many black people may wonder why I'm spilling my guts. Sometimes even the giving of a part of oneself crosses the fine line and becomes a burden to the hearer. As Flip Wilson exclaimed, rejecting the burden of presumptions, "*You* don't know me!" Some may wonder why anyone who looks white would take on such a burden. And some may tell me, and have, that they already knew I was black before I said a word. And may say, in fact, that they don't think I look white at all. "Why do you think you look white?" a woman asked me after a reading. I remember how once a woman had come up to me after a reading and said that she understood exactly what I was talking about, because she looked white and always had the same experiences. But she was dark and had wide features and kinky hair. Did she really see herself as white-looking? Did she appear more black to me than she actually was? Did others see her in a different way than I did?

After a recent dinner party for my mother, my black friends astonished me by saying that I look whiter than she does. But I had always thought she looked whiter than I. Was that my way of rejecting her, of not wanting to be like her? Or was it my way of "ennobling" what I came from? Or have the two of us changed? Someone said by way of explanation that you get darker as you age. And somebody else said that something about me looks "blacker" than I used to look, perhaps because of something I do or say. My face *does* look different, as if the bones of my blackness have risen up to the surface. So even the self is liquid; it shifts slightly. How can we tell, when reality has been so twisted, what we see? A woman in the audience said I'd better have a good, clear picture on my book; she said that, in a way, it is brave of me to say I look white, because saying you look white, at least to some black people, is a red flag of presumption, arrogance, and perhaps even insanity.

"She think she white" was one of the worst insults hurled from childhood, rasped nearly out of the subject's hearing. Language and body have to contort themselves in order to embody the painful meanings of double consciousness. Often black people can only say in tone, in nuance, in the set of the mouth, or in the shifting of the eyes what language alone cannot say. Perhaps because of the ambivalence we feel about language, we must put the body itself to use. The hearer must pay attention, take in with all the senses, so that the act of speaking and hearing moves closer, like a dance that must be entered into with one's whole being. There is no dictionary to refer to. Perhaps every word we have uttered since slavery has in it that tension between possibility and doubt, language twisted like a horrible face—the tension from which art itself arises.

"She think she white" was said with a bitterness, irony, disgust, and even a humor that only one raised with generations of historical pain can understand. It was not only a judgment, it was a punishment as well, for it embodied the consequence of exile, of exclusion. Suddenly the accused had stepped outside of love, community, and entered that territory in another person's head that made her the thing hated.

It may have been something in the way the accused moved her head—flipping her hair?—or that she appeared to be trying to make friends with a white person.

"She think she white" was an accusation that you had to think ahead of, to watch what you did in every manner. It might indicate, not that you wore a pretty dress, but that you wore it in a certain way, as if you were proud of it as a fact of your being, as if you deserved it, took it as a personal accomplishment, as if in some way it created a hardness around you, set you apart, gave you not only an identity of your own but one that separated you from the others and shut them out. The smell of exclusion brought quick reprisal. As members of an oppressed community, we were by necessity dependent on each other.

"She think she white" implied: "Yes, we know that in our society it is better to be white, but we have to constantly monitor that desire. If not, we may threaten the very foundation of our community, our trust and dependence on each other." "She think she white" seemed to guard a little sacred territory in the speaker's mind, a final defense against self-rejection, questioning the accused's sanity rather than one's own. It suggested that the speaker may feel angry not only about being abandoned but about being abandoned in a place that she has mixed feelings about in the first place. For if one were totally happy being black, why would anger come out at someone else's pretension?

"She think she white" is not the same as "She wants to be white." It means, she think she *is* white. It aims not only to make the hearer think that they have done something wrong, but to assault the very idea of the self, to deal a shattering blow to the center of all thought, the self as perception. Isn't that racism's greatest injury?

Carla Gary told this story: She and her family had moved into a middle-class neighborhood when she was five. They were the only black family. She loved her new house and was perfectly happy. The first day at the local playground, she heard a little girl screaming and running out of the playground, "The nigger is going to get me, the nigger is going to get me." Carla looked around. She didn't know what a nigger was, and the sound of the little girl's voice terrified her. She, too, began to run and scream, "The nigger is going to get me," right behind the little white girl, who was looking over her shoulder in astonishment and running even faster. Carla ran all the way home. "The nigger is going to get me," she called out to her mother. Her mother sat down and tried to calm her, laughing, but with tears in her eyes.

"Carla," she said, "you *are* the nigger."

"No I'm not," Carla insisted.

"Yes, Carla, it's you, you're the nigger."

Carla said she could not imagine that she could be that thing that the girl was running from, that thing that had elicited such a scream. Certainly she could not be that thing.

What does one do with an incomprehensible fact? What kind of brain must be created and shaped to contain it?

"She think she white" is an accusation beyond race. It means, "She's crazy!"

Among black people craziness has always been seen as one of the most feared realities. Just the mention of therapy to some black people causes a visceral response: "I don't want nobody messing with my mind." It's about trust, I think. A sense that one works things out with one's friends or family, with people one knows personally rather than with people one pays money to listen. But I think it also means let sleeping dogs lie, expressing the fear of unearthing buried disappointments, losses, and angers. Perhaps the mind so held in place is really a stopgap that mustn't be tampered with.

Once, when I was about eight or nine, I was snooping among my loved aunt's drawers. She had earned the reputation for giving all of her beautiful and priceless treasures away to those she loved, so that often on a summer afternoon I would snoop through her drawers and closet for something to thieve. I didn't need to ask; just wearing her ring on my finger or taking money out of her drawer entitled me to ownership. One afternoon I took a chair and climbed up to her closet shelf. There were hatboxes with possible treasures. I opened them and a foul odor emerged, a complex ripeness. There were napkins with used blood wrapped carefully in toilet paper, dozens placed in a circular design, the way I supposed ritual objects were placed in ancient tombs. In my aunt's immaculate house, I had discovered a terrible secret that, of course, I must never ask about. Was she saving some part of her self? She had had a child who died shortly after birth. Was this a kind of mourning? It may have been around the time of her menopause. Was she holding on to the last precious drops of blood? I had been taught we were to get rid of the dirty evidence, but I could never tell if that was because of its "badness," or because of its power. Perhaps the taboo was there as a marker, to remind us of exactly what we must *not* get rid of, what we had to hide or it would be taken away.

This woman who so loved us, who sheltered our family in her home for years, for nothing, who gave every hard thing she worked her whole life for away. "Bread on the water always comes home," she'd say.

Years later, after her children left, she accused her husband of keeping a woman in the basement, a "whore" who slept and lived in the coal cellar. She knew this hideous, blacked-out woman had been upstairs because, when she came home from work, there was evidence—her cold creams were missing, or somehow she had poisoned them so that my aunt's face broke out in rashes, eczema, and sores.

Out of loneliness and stale desires were forced up textures, smells, voices whispering and laughing in the kitchen, kitchen shelves lined with mattress ticking, cabinets, starched and ironed sheets, the meat of the bodies that I loved, the women, cut open, sewn back together, ugly to themselves, even though young, curly-headed, gloriously smelling of human sleep, baby pee, and frustration, and always the intense effort to be loved.

There are those who say, "Speak the unspeakable," "Tell the truth, it is the writer's job to say," but it occurs to me that any held reality retains a power, that perhaps silence is a way of protecting what it is not yet time to bring to light.

I think of the powerlessness of those black women, their only worth as servants, their bodies, their sex, a commodity on the open market. There was the slow retreat of hope, a way of carrying yourself on your back, encased, like a bad history you can't get out of, so that everything, every beauty on the earth became secondary: a life too late to be claimed. For these women the most powerful weapon might have been the one that no one knew about, that no one could find. Perhaps against everything I have learned as a writer, there is something I have learned as a child of the oppressed—there is a secret place that, once articulated, becomes banal and squalid.

An excerpt from my mother's book, *Bread on the Waters,* chapter entitled "My Sister Eleanora":

When I remember the gentle way that my sister endured years of sickness: heart disease, hypertension, and the relentless, painful arthritis that gradually eroded and deformed her limbs, how she masked the pain, rather than inflict it on others, the daily agony of watching her physical beauty worn away and her movements hampered . . .

When I think of her lifelong selflessness and the unselfishness in small things, in large things; her abundant love of others and how she gladly shared all that she ever had.

When I think of the racial injustices and indignities in the business world that she bore; how she labored all her working years for a pittance of what white professionals at the same level, but of lesser talent and productivity, made. I laugh when I recall that Eleanora wasn't in the habit of crying "foul." She'd take a hard look at the hand she had been dealt, then play it for all it was worth. Trumping white aces with satisfaction and glee.

When I think of all these things, then I think that surely my sister Eleanora was a saint.

Not that she was without faults or blemishes. No, she had her human share. So did the saints. Faithless Thomas. Adulterous Magdalene. Lying Peter. Complaining Martha.

In a different setting she could have been a Mother Teresa, roaming the world, administering to the poor. Had she been born white with the advantages and opportunities her talents and industry merited, she could have been a wealthy advertising giant giving away her fortune to better the world.

Eleanora did not "grow old gracefully," as the saying goes. Forced into early retirement (as other senior employees subsequently were) by a new, inept, and desperate management, she never recovered from the blow. Neither did Annis Furs, which, now rudderless, without Mr. Annis and the old spirit of employees steeped in his tradition, tarnished its one-hundred-year image; went from a seven-story, first-class, reputable fur emporium to a small, dark suite in an off-the-beaten-track building and from thence into obscurity.

In later years, when I looked at her reddish, puffed hands and feet, still busy, going, doing, my insides would turn over and I'd cry out, "Oh, Sis, let me help you."

"Don't worry," she'd answer, "I'll just throw it out of my mind." That was her free, self-administered therapy. Just throw it out of my mind.

She died alone, in a hospital where she had been admitted two days earlier for medical tests only. Victim of a tired, indifferent doctor and a could-care-less hospital staff. Even as I ran crazily through darkened corridors that night, I could hear in the distance the eerie sound CODE BLUE. CODE BLUE. Good-bye, Sis. It was a gray night, 12 December 1979. Mama had died on the same date of the same month, forty-four years before.

From her thirties, Eleanora's companion had been pain. While time lined her baby-face, her step grew unsteady and her self-confidence wavered. The ravages of sickness, partial loss of physical independence, and the secret dream birds that through the years had flown away, all converged upon her and left an anxious woman with fears she could never lay hands on. Sometimes I thought they were ghosts of her own life's unnoticed and unmet needs.

She had no professional counselor to guide her, no talk shows to enlighten her, no support group, no "how-to" books to help her deal with the harsh realities of her day, to understand the later physical and emotional pressures that beset her. In the "me" generation, she was out of place—for she could never learn to live for herself.

I think of the young doctors, lawyers, artists, business

executives, and all the others, the many who may never have heard her name, who live the good life now, because at some point then, during the bad times, Eleanora was there for their parents and grandparents.

African-American people of today have many heroines of yesterday, sung and unsung, famous and forgotten. . . .

For several months, as I sat talking to my therapist, I would suddenly sense myself inside of my own body. It was a kind of flash event, and I don't know how to talk about it, because I don't usually experience myself as outside of myself. I experience myself as feeling quite normal. But it was as if, like lightning, I became aware that I had slipped back inside of my body, and realized, therefore, that the rest of the time I must not be, that most of the time I am my own watcher.

Being myself felt strange and wonderful, as if I were conscious of something I didn't yet know how to operate, a human machine I didn't yet know how to drive. I looked down at my legs and they seemed so big, my feet seemed enormous, gargantuan. Looking over at the therapist, I seemed to take up the whole side of the room. I felt like Alice in Wonderland, my head brushing the ceiling.

Another time I felt small, powerless, and the therapist seemed large. "Seemed" isn't quite the right word. I knew our size was the same size as before, but I'm talking about a sensed reality, something between a hallucination and a waking dream. It was as if my psyche's sense of myself was in the process of changing, as if I had caught it right as it was forming itself, as I was sitting in that chair talking, I was liquid and plastic.

In the past few weeks, I have had a sensation of

being more inside of myself. I have gotten several lovely colored pens that feel good in my hand and I enjoy writing, enjoy forming the letters. I have always been one who got D's in handwriting. I hurry over the event, as if the form of the letters isn't important, as if I'm not important, as if I am not living now, but in some future attainment.

I hurry over eating, cooking, and cleaning, as if I am hurrying my unimportant life away, as if there is something in the future that I will get to that will make me feel important. My father called me "careless" when I lost the keys. So much of my life has been "careless" of me.

What if that feeling of separation and distance from the "other" is fear of being one with the self, a fear to take in emotionally the meaning of a part of the self that one is not yet ready to handle?

My therapist says that children who have been abused deaden their feelings. My husband asks me what it is like. It's as if I'm outside myself, getting the message of what I've done an instant later. As if I'm watching myself, telling myself what to do.

I had a dream two nights ago in which a toddler was told by her parents that she had to massage the heart of a dog that was dying. I was wondering how the parents could expect that child to take on such a responsibility, to resuscitate the dying. In fact, it seemed certain to me that the dog would die, and yet I stood by and watched, letting the child massage the heart, as if I didn't have enough will to relieve the child of that burden. Perhaps some part of me still hoped the parents were right, that the child could do the impossible, though I thought how terrible it would be if the dog died and the child thought it was her fault. The dog did die. I remember feeling that inconsolable wound that the child must feel, that she had done something wrong, that she was inadequate and had failed, and that her whole life would be haunted. I was so angry at my parents—I realized now the parents were *mine*—for putting that sense of guilt and responsibility on that child—who must have been me.

I held the child and comforted her. I said you aren't to blame, there is nothing you could have done. After the dream I thought perhaps all is not lost for that child, because she, unlike me was when I was a child, has me to take care of her. Now I am her parent.

Sometimes I see a black person who, to me, truly is *not* black anymore. And I don't mean that they don't have a certain kind of hair or features, that they are middle class or rich or light or educated. I mean it feels as if their "soul" had died. Their skin may be as dark as mahogany, but there is some evil I sense, an evil that comes of losing a great battle in the self to accept and love all its parts, even the parts most hated by this world.

Last night I bought a calla lily. I don't know why. As I was walking through the garage of the local shopping center where I had stopped to buy a vase, a young black girl approached me. "Is that a calla lily?" she asked.

And in the china shop, as I was squatting on the floor trying to find a vase tall enough, a woman bent over me, "That is such a beautiful flower," she said, a middle-aged woman with her white-haired mother.

Has my face grown open as a flower, so that one can approach me without fear? Can the frightened drop their defenses at the sight of me?

Rick, the Cabdriver

Last year, after I came back from my trip to Africa, I got into the cab with a driver whom I had come to rely on. He had always been on time when I had called, and he had also lived in New York for many years, so we had fun talking about restaurants and New York while going to and from the airport for several months. He said, "How was Africa?" and I felt that little shiver of danger.

There always comes a time that seems to be the right time to reveal it. However, what does one say? Should I have suddenly broken into this conversation with, "Oh by the way, I'm black." Though I had ridden in the car with him for months, there really hadn't been any conversation we had had that had come close to being a right time. Now, however, perhaps it was going to be too late to do it without a great deal of discomfort for both of us.

I tried to control the conversation by giving him the "approved" version of my trip. "We visited the palace of an African king," I said, to which he replied, laughing, "And did you see the fools?!"

I had two choices: Tell him I am black and that his comment offended me, or not tell him I am black, continue to be "the university professor," and enter into a debate with him about his opinions. I decided to continue to be "the university professor," because it occurred to me that as soon as he found out I was black he would have just discounted whatever I said: "Oh, you know how sensitive they are," or "Well, here's another one of those nigger fools." We fought all the way to the airport. And it felt good. It was wonderful to be able to fight him without constantly have to get out of the way of the racism in his mind. That's when I realized that it is much easier for white people to confront racism than it is for blacks. Because no matter what a white person says or does about racism, they are still white, which gives them the privilege of being listened to without having already been judged as doubly unreliable—unreliable because they are black and, therefore, foolish, and unreliable because they are merely acting defensively, defending their own race. And I don't just mean that that burden exists because of what is in white people's minds. When I was arguing with that cabdriver, I was relieved of the burden of being black in my *own* mind. What a privilege that seemed to be, not to have to be black in my own mind!

When I told this story at a black college where I was reading that weekend, a young black woman in the audience was furious at me. I had asked the audience if they thought my objective to be heard by the cab-driver justified my not "admitting" that I was black. (One of the other burdens of race is feeling guilty about and responsible for the discomfort in other people's minds.) She said for me to escape the pain while others are not able to made me a betrayer. The next time I rode with the cabdriver, I felt I had to tell him. And it seemed even harder—as if I were admitting I had been a liar, though, really, I hadn't been. But silence, as you can see, is just as "wrong" for me.

I told him I was black. I told him why I hadn't told him before. And I told him why I was telling him now—that it was just as important for me to say as it was for him to hear. He apologized and he seemed sincere. He repeated he wasn't a racist. I tried to be nice, but after these kinds of revelations and arguments, a part of me recedes, as if I have been beaten up, mostly by myself, and I don't want to be reminded.

That night he called me to apologize again. I was extremely moved, but I didn't call him anymore when I wanted a cab. I didn't want to face that past, I didn't want to have to get over it, I didn't want to feel responsible for forgiving him, for being a "different" black person, for continuing to educate or not educate, or any of it. I don't want to be responsible for white people. And, in fact, why not give my money to a black cabdriver?

A few weeks ago I saw him as I was coming out of the airport. I was loaded down with bags, and he turned back, as if he had sensed me back there, and he stared me in the face. I was glad to see him, though I couldn't at first remember who he was. I felt that discomfort that I often feel when I wake up in the morning, when I used to go into the bathroom and see Bruce for the first time, when I'd hesitate to speak because I wanted to see if he was angry at me for something I'd done wrong. Given any blank situation, I suppose, the first thing I impose on it is my own guilt.

Now that I have nearly given up on my marriage, I am grieving the loss. All those years of indecision, of trying! But coming this close to ending it makes me realize the fragile and sad beauties of our long relationship.

For years, when I would get up in the morning, after saying terrible things to him the night before, after assaulting him with threats of divorce, saying how unhappy I was with him, I would get up nearly slinking to the room in which I would greet him, the bathroom, which I was both drawn to yet wanted to avoid. Inside, there was a gold light, like the little shelter in a chapel. I could have used the other bathroom, but I didn't. I would come in with an angry look on my face (I have allowed myself as an adult to have a reputation for getting up in a bad mood, though when I was a baby, everyone said I always woke up singing!) Perhaps I would come in hiding, slunk down on one side in my body, avoiding his gaze, as if I had become something alien during the night, as if my breath had grown tentacles or my mashed hair had caved in the side of my head; as if being forgotten, forgetting him, swimming in my own dreams, made me unworthy not only of his love but even to be seen.

For many years I'd come in not daring to be hopeful, for many, many years—perhaps all of our years together, nearly thirty years of marriage—each morning dreading the look of disgust in his eyes. I knew it would happen eventually. I had a hard shell over my body so that he couldn't see the frightened, anxious thing that lived under there, shivering like a little rat. What I remember is his first smile in the morning as he was shaving, seeing me walk in the door. Looking at me over his razor again and stopping a second to smile and greet me and then dunking the razor under the water again. It was always the same smile, a new smile, a look that didn't acknowledge or even remember what had happened the night before, as if there had been nothing said, in spite of the vitriol that had come pouring out of me. He always looked up as if he wasn't going to throw me away, hate me. Everything was new and could begin again.

Some mornings something in me couldn't admit how soft I am, how much I had felt wrong and sad and frightened, how much I needed his forgetfulness. I wanted to buttress the self that still seemed hard and briny. I would answer gruffly out of the corner of my mouth. (It is dangerous to let them know you care. It can make them feel too powerful. Then they turn you away.)

Even that halfhearted greeting didn't seem to bother him. He went on shaving. Often he would be humming some excruciatingly boring song—the Michigan fight song—so that I couldn't be sure if his kindness was meant for me, or if he was just completely unaware, stupid, so insensitive that even his kindness happened in a closed room in which I didn't even exist. Perhaps it was a way of shutting me out, of ignoring me. How can you be sure of love, or hatred, or anything?

Sometimes, like a little frightened child, I'd need to ask if he was angry. Sometimes I couldn't find the words, and I'd ask him for a hug, and perhaps he'd turn and wipe his hands and put his arms around me. He'd do that even today if I asked. He never refused a hug, that small but immense human bond. That was a good enough reason to stay with him—thirty years of marriage and ten more of friendship, forty years— that was enough reason to bear the lack of touch, the lack of desire, the lack of reaching out, the holding back, the lack of time, conversation, the lack of everything that finally scorched the bottom of my soul.

At a recent reading, when I told the story about the cabdriver, about not calling him again, a white woman in the audience was angry. Why did you do that? She wanted me to forgive.

When do you lie down like a rug and take it? When do you accept them back and forget? Can you forget it? Or must you carry it around like a saint, acting as if you're not angry. Forgiveness is the last thing to come. Especially forgiveness of your self.

Suddenly, coming home from a long trip, loaded down with bags, I saw Rick, the cabdriver I hadn't called in almost a year. Seeing him had a warm feeling attached to it, even before I recognized who he was, like seeing an old friend. In spite of that instant when I felt I had done something wrong, I had turned into something ugly, that I couldn't make the right connection, I was still glad.

"Can you drive me home?" I asked.

"No," he said, "I can't take over somebody else's job," and he pointed to the line of cabs waiting. But he wasn't saying it because he was angry. I could tell. "But maybe if I tell them you're my special customer . . ." he added, and I parked my bags and waited.

It took a long time. He had to ask, then go back to the parking lot, which was blocks away, and I watched him go back and I waited there on the curb wondering if I should have just let him go, that maybe this was too much. . . . Maybe I had gone overboard by asking if he could take me, the way I often ask for too much just to cover up my own fear and amazement.

Finally, he was back and helped me into the cab, and we went on just as before, as if none of the past had happened. Once during the ride he astounded me by figuring out how to ask why I hadn't called him. It wasn't with an accusation or by making me feel guilty, but by something delicate and subtle that allowed me to explain that I'd been taking myself to the airport, that I had brought my car from Maryland, and that I had been saving myself some money. Telling him that made me realize that it was true. I hadn't betrayed our friendship or been unable to take the past. My not seeing him, in spite of what I had thought, was really based on practical concerns, not on our conversation about race at all. I hadn't been cold and unforgiving.

I was glad he had figured out a way to ask me, and I remembered why I had liked him to be my cab-driver, how he was bright, quick to notice things and respond, that he said what was on his mind and that his sizing up of things was usually protective in some kind of way and right. Amazing how you can tell such things and trust, in a deep way, a cabdriver!

Our meetings may resume again next year. Certainly I'll try to call him if I need a cab. If he has the same number. If I'm at home, where I've kept his phone number in my drawer. I have no fear that either one of us can't take it. "Time heals all wounds," my father always said. It wasn't until many years after his death that I realized he meant the wounds that he himself had inflicted.

Tony's Bus Special

On the way to a workshop in South Jersey, I meet Tony, a seventy-five-year-old man who goes down to Atlantic City to shoot craps. I notice that they all know each other on the bus. Everyone is a retiree. They tell me it's a "free" day. You pay seventeen dollars for the bus ticket, get back five-fifty for your lunch and seven dollars to play the machines. "Some people go just to walk on the boardwalk. It's better than staying at home," he says.

I haven't been on the bus for five minutes before the group starts talking about who their favorite driver is. "I like the colored girl," a woman says. "She's good."

"Not 'colored,'" Tony corrects her. "Black. Black or white."

Two minutes later he turns to me. "What are you?"

"Black," I answer.

He looks blank, as if I hadn't said anything.

"Black," I try again.

Now he looks as if he got a fly caught in his ear and he has to knock it out. "What?" he asks. "Black? No," he answers himself.

"I know what I am."

"Which one, your mother or father?"

"Both," I say.

"I bet your father was surprised when he saw you!"

"No," I say. "Both my parents look just like me."

"Somebody got in there somewhere," he explains to himself.

Then he goes go on to talk about the best spaghetti sauce in the world, his grandmother's, and he gives me the recipe, and names it "Tony's Bus Special Spaghetti Sauce." He makes me guess his grandmother's secret.

"Sugar," I say, and he makes a deadly face. "The wine vinegar cuts the acid," he says.

Then he shows me something I'll never see again, no matter if I live another forty years. He says he discovered it himself, by accident, "just like Thomas Edison."

He folds a page of a newspaper and tears it in strips. He asks me if I've been a good girl and want to go to heaven, and if I have somebody in my family who's been bad. Then he opens one of the strips and hands me a cross and tells me to hand that to Saint Peter. He opens up the other and produces, letter by letter, "hell" and drapes it over the back of the bus seat. "Tell the bad one to give Saint Peter this."

TONY'S BUS SPECIAL SPAGHETTI SAUCE

1 can paste	1 tbs. oil
1 can sauce	2 leaves basil
1 large can plum tomatoes	2 cloves crushed garlic
1 oz. wine vinegar	salt and pepper

Simmer for at least three hours.

You can cut up and add baby back ribs or neck bones. Fry them until the grease is gone. Simmer them with the sauce for the last fifteen minutes. Or you can add meatballs.

MEATBALLS

Pork, veal, beef, parsley, Parmesan, 2 eggs, garlic, salt and pepper, bread crumbs

What Makes You Black?

For all practical purposes "race" is not so much a biological phenomenon as a social myth. UNESCO

It is always a question asked by whites who, I suppose, think, looking at me, that the necessary attributes—color, features, hair, or perhaps something more subtle, speech, some giveaway inflection of being—are missing. Some have said, shocked: But nothing about you is black! It expresses a puzzlement, a curiosity, but it can also be an accusation, as if they were saying: Look, now, black is one thing that I am absolutely sure of—you owe me an explanation! They yearn to make identity solid, to give it a nose or an ear or an eye. A nurse from the South in one of my creative writing classes wrote about how, in the hospital she worked at in Georgia, there was a series of procedures posted on the nursery wall for babies of indeterminate race, among them a procedure to measure the size of its genitals.

Black people never ask. We understand that blackness is both real and unreal, that it can't be explained, nailed down, or verified. That it is an attribute out of the body, slightly, like a halo and therefore insubstantial. It may be guessed at or ascertained, but even when it is not, that doesn't mean that it is not possible, or even unlikely.

"You bright?" a young girl asked me as she passed by on a street in the small town in Louisiana that was my mother's childhood home. We had come to see my grandmother's grave and the estate where she had worked as the cook and head domestic for fifteen years. I had never heard it said that way before. "Bright?" I asked.

The sudden understanding of what she had asked is

probably what makes me black, more so than my body. "Yes," I answered, smiling, before she offered another word.

My mother told me that as you get older you change, not just your body, but what's inside; you become another person. I remember from childhood with what eagerness we took in anyone who even slightly and for any reason trembled toward us—Ava Gardner because of the way she moved, talked, because of her mouth and her green—hybrid characteristic: sign of the islands—eyes. Perhaps there was the smoke of some actual gossip, but we said it as if there wasn't a question. It isn't exactly that we believe in the identity that has been foisted on us—their one-drop rule, the idea that one drop of black blood in your ancestry makes you black. Rather, maybe we are like the kindest occupants of the poorest house who, nevertheless, are eager to open our doors and let any supplicant in. Maybe it is a way of expressing our loneliness, or a desire to bring what we suspect closer, to make it real—that really, deep down, we are all, if the truth be known, benefactors of that somewhere, someplace nigger in the woodpile.

My uncle said they know we're better, that's why they all want a suntan and a perm. My aunt said that our family had so many problems because of all those warring bloods in us.

That girl who called me bright. . . . Did she recognize me because I looked so comfortable, so happy in front of the door of that ninety-four-year-old woman who had held the wake in her living room for my grandmother when she died, when my poor mother was eighteen. "Chère," she called me as we did dishes, she slowly going around the saucers with a little gray rag, and me slowly drying.

"Miss Cora," I had asked her, a woman who raised

four children alone, her husband having died in an accident when she was in her thirties, "did you get what you wanted?"

"Chère," she answered, thoughtfully, "I ain't never wanted for *nothin'*."

Was it something in my body that gave me away? That girl, with her Southern X-ray eyes, having peered more deeply and concertedly into miscegenation. She looked proud of herself, as if she had caught me hiding. Or perhaps she was smiling because it made her happy to find me kin. Or perhaps, like those girls who combed and brushed my "good" hair, she saw me as an example of what *could* in fact burst out of any one of us girls—not the "throwback" our mothers warned us about, making us worry all through our pregnancies, and check first, before fingers and toes, our baby's ears—but a "bright" child, like *me*.

I realized this morning, after my interview with a woman from a newspaper, that one of my biggest strengths as a writer, perhaps the only really unique thing I can give, is that I am determined to tell the truth. I think that most people protect themselves, their relationships, their friends, by not quite facing the worst. On the contrary, I go searching for it. Especially in myself. I keep telling the truth even when it is abhorrent. I have a drive to break the secrets, because I think that what we don't tell others, we often lie to ourselves about. I am determined not to lie to myself.

I don't know why it is that we fear others' thoughts so. It seemed especially true of the black middle-class people in my childhood. It seemed that it was so important to keep up appearances, to not let people know there were problems, as if problems meant we were failures. I am sure that years of conditioning in a society that blamed us for our own destruction—they're animals, they don't deserve any better—being aware of what power white people's thoughts had over our lives, made us feel especially vulnerable. If we controlled our anger, were kind, responsible, dressed in good clothes, drove expensive cars, racism would not affect us. But then there is always the story of the black middle-class doctor stopped in an all-white suburb because the police thought his car was stolen. It seems that many of the shames and desires of the black middle class had at their base a desire to change the perception of whites. This is not just a hangover from slavery, it is an accurate assessment of the danger in the world we live in today. Just about every black person I ever met has some tale of arbitrary cruelty.

Perhaps the only reason I can "get past" certain fears is because of my light skin. Perhaps even my insistence on being relaxed about clothing is not an indication of an admirable lack of materialism, but rather the symbol of one who hasn't needed to use material things as a self-defense. Perhaps even my digging into myself and telling the "truth" means something different than if I were a dark-skinned person. Perhaps in our world I am protected and dark-skinned people are vulnerable in ways I cannot even imagine.

I met a large, dark woman in a workshop for black women who told the story of the day she got sick of them following her in the drugstore, the record store, as if she were a thief. That afternoon she went to the hairdresser to have her hair straightened, to the same man who had pressed her hair for years. She sat in the chair with her money in her hand, and what went through her mind was how all those years—since she was a baby—every time her mother straightened her hair, she thought to herself, *I wish my hair was straight*, and suddenly, she was tired of that wish. "Shave it off," she said.

He was shocked. "You don't mean it." This huge woman whose hair I suppose he thought was her one good attribute. . . .

"Shave it off."

She said when he cut off her hair, years of heaviness went with it. She felt lighter, lifted. Now, even though she's followed, looked at, examined, until sometimes she has to confront—"What are *you* looking at?"—she feels better.

In one way, she is utterly free; yet in another, she is chained, like an entranced demon who must roam the earth howling out in terrible pain until one person does an act of kindness.

She did not seem to be a happy woman. Obviously her choice was not a victory that many of us would accept. But we understood, looking at her, the bravery of her act, which put our own puny complaints into perspective. She had cut off a part of herself.

The division of the human species into "races" is partly conventional and partly arbitrary and does not imply any hierarchy whatsoever. . . . Racial divisions have limited scientific interest and may even carry the risk of inviting abusive generalization. . . . The human problems arising from so-called "race" relations are social in origin rather than biological. . . . Racism falsely claims that there is a scientific basis for arranging groups hierarchically that are immutable and innate. . . .

UNESCO

Recently I found that a white woman in a workshop I was conducting in Alaska had grown up at about the same time and just a few miles from my husband's hometown in Ohio. We began to talk about the similarities between those two small towns—each had two black families, a "good" black family and a "bad" black family. I could tell from her conversation and writings that she was very interested in examining some of her connections to the past, and I was, at the end of my twenty-five-year marriage, interested in exploring and coming to terms with some of the most painful aspects of my marriage, which I was sure had a great deal to do with the fear, anger, and repression my husband had felt as a member of the "good" family in his town. I suggested an experiment that I hoped would give us both enough structure to open up and go beyond what we had already accepted as "truth."

"Let's collaborate on a piece about those towns," I suggested. "You write and I'll write and we'll just go back and forth like that."

She said, "I can't do that. I'm intimidated by you!" I encouraged her to write whatever came to her and she sat down. Immediately she began writing—most fearfully—about her early experiences with the black girl in her class, Barbara, who intimidated her physically, who called out after her, "Amy throws her ass around." She had connected me to her.

We began writing in twenty-minute blocks and sharing our small pieces. Soon we were spending whole days together, me working at her kitchen table while she wrote upstairs, then lying out in the cool spring sunshine on her glassed-in porch that looked out on the sparkling waters and majestic mountains of Kachemac Bay, and talking.

Hearing her pieces about what it was like growing up in that town, what it was like for her and for the black children—she remembered that the "grabby" black boy, unlike the "grabby" white boys, was beaten publicly with a belt as he went up the stairs. The white boys were merely scolded. I began to touch some of the pain of a man who has had to be perfectly emotionally controlled. His mother had admonished him to put his energy into work, to stay away from the white girls. Just fifty miles away black boys had been lynched. I began to see how our most intimate relationships, our own abilities to love, express ourselves, and indeed to live, are deeply and permanently affected by racism. I began to experience the sorrow of what we can't change in ourselves—though it brings great harm to us and those we love.

And Amy began to see how her relationship with the black children in her school was, in a way, set up by what she had come to school prepared to experience and feel—that she had been intimidated by her father, unprotected by her mother, and that pattern of psychological abuse continued not only through school but through many adult relationships. Barbara had been merely the instrument put in an expected place. Through her exploration, through her painful writing, she began to see that, in spite of the fact she thought she was open-minded, tolerant, she had racist attitudes. She began to understand how racism sets us all up to see the world in a way that keeps the same destructive patterns happening. One teacher, the only person in her childhood who had encouraged her and praised her mental abilities, told her, in the most sympathetic voice, that she had discouraged a black girl in her class from studying to be a secretary. "I told her that in a town with problems like this, it would be impossible." Amy knew that this woman was not just passing on caring information. She was perpetuating an unjust circumstance. However, because she was the only person in her whole life who had encouraged her, she said nothing.

Because of her writing, she came to have compassion for herself, the victim of a sexually repressive and authoritarian family, and compassion for those black children. For all her beliefs that they had been the ones with fearful powers, she remembered with great sadness that the black children in the town were absent when she went on to high school and college.

Can whites begin to understand and take in the pain of this racist society? So often white people, when a deep pain with regard to racism is uncovered, want it to be immediately addressed, healed, released. Black people have had to live with the wounds of racism for generations. Even goodwill and hard work won't make the personal hurts cease. If this book has any purpose, it's to show the persistence of internal conflicts, of longing, shame, and terror. It represents a twenty-year obsession to observe myself when these feelings arise, rather than to deny or repress them. I have found that there is no cure. Perhaps awareness can give us a second to contain, so that we do not pass these damages on to others.

A friend who lives in St. Croix sent me a drawing of a Cruzan woman, a dark woman in her seventies, tall, wiry, and strong. She is standing at a gate in front of an old broken-down shack with a tin roof. She has on what appears to be her Sunday suit—plain and threadbare, but worn with a look of self-sufficiency and pride. She looks as if she is getting ready to walk out of the gate, out of the picture into the world, her face with a look of self-acceptance and acceptance of the one she is looking at—who, fortunately, happens to be me!

Everything about her is an expression of a wisdom that has not come easily. We stare at each other across that gulf between life and art and she conveys a healing dignity, a serenity and grace. She mirrors something in my deepest soul that has remained silent and covered in the way that the statues are covered during Lent, when the church is in mourning and draped in purple. I meditate on her face every day, trying to duplicate internally every line and crease. I have read that in meditation one is transformed into the thing that one meditates on. She is my Goddess, the first outward manifestation of my own black divinity. All my life, since my years of Catholic school, I have thought of God as a white man and unlike me. Now, after fifty years, I understand the importance of finding and inventing those internal mirrors in which we see ourselves as sacred.

Face to Face

There are so many truths about race that remain unvoiced, hidden, perhaps because, voiced, they would unlock our pain and our hearts would flood open and be changed.

A light-skinned woman told me this story. One day she was in a group of black women and told them how black men often call out sexual comments when she passes them by, and that when she rebuffs them, they frequently call her names and make rude remarks— "Bitch, you think you cute." She told the women how angry it makes her to be the object of these men's harassment and abuse. The women chided her. They had not had such experiences and they didn't know what she was talking about.

Were they telling her that they doubted her perceptions? Did it make her wonder what was wrong with her? Did she think that for some reason they had aligned themselves against her, perhaps because black women feel they should protect their men? Did she feel isolated and let down?

She looked around the room and realized that she was the only light-skinned woman present. Maybe what the women were reporting was true, maybe black men *hadn't* called out such remarks to them. Maybe, trained as we all have been to admire a certain kind of "beauty," many black men found light-skinned women more attractive, or maybe they felt more comfortable calling out such remarks to light-skinned women, thinking that they were fair game and could be harassed with impunity. Or maybe the women were lying, defending black men because they didn't trust or like *her*. But she couldn't say any of this ·

because of the history of distrust between light women and dark.

She was afraid the women would have been pained to think that many black men aren't as attracted to them, and afraid that even asking the question would cause a greater chasm. Are darker women "missing" something? And is what they are missing, perhaps, not entirely a bad thing? Could the women talk about the complexity of this issue? Or would they quickly retreat behind barriers of suspicion and pain? After so many years in which light-skinned women have had privileges and often been responsible for much hurt done to dark women, perhaps they could not talk about it with empathy for each other's point of view. Is it possible that they could recognize the pain of those black men? How they have had to deny a part of their own blackness in order to absorb the idea of what is beautiful and desirable in our culture, that they are running away from a part of themselves, and that what they are running toward, they obviously have very mixed feelings about—both attraction to as well as hatred for and rage. Should we be silent and not arouse these ghosts: the accusation that light women think they are "cute," that we steal and have stolen darker women's men? Will the light woman be silent and go away distrusting her own perception, feeling more aware of her difference?

None of us are winners. Once again we are not really able to get down to the real thing, to see what makes our pain different, and then to go past that, to see what makes our pain the same. Audre Lorde asked, "Why must we always be first against each other?" Because we are that close, because there is that much anger and hurt, and because it is so hard to find the real source, so difficult to reach back in history.

Our truths divide us. We fear speaking to each other, black and white, light and dark, men and women, rich and poor. Yet it is possible to see the context, how we have all been the victims, how it has damaged us.

We are afraid of saying the wrong thing. Of making things worse. Of proving that we really are as bad, stupid, or wrong as we suspect the other one thinks. Yet our silence makes us not trust our perceptions, not trust ourselves, and in the long run, it keeps us "safe," unthreatened, but stops the really important movement of change through us. The inner structures with all their defenses must tumble.

Sometimes I dread reading my work, not only because I'm afraid black people will hate me for voicing these fears and inner conflicts, but because I wonder if, like me, most others prefer not to think of what is causing them pain. Here I am reminding them. What a terrible knowledge for our children. We close our mouths. We inspire. We wait until they can take it. Or we say nothing and let them find out for themselves, slowly, as we found out, walking through the world often alone, without our parents' interpretations, that heaviness that we keep praying has changed. It is too much to speak of. We say, "I don't want to make them paranoid, to make them go around with a chip on their shoulders."

Things don't change. *Newsweek*, October 1994— blacks have inferior intelligence, re: *The Bell Curve.* It's as if, no matter how much I heal myself, the world keeps breaking my image into shards and sticking them into my heart. I am supposed to distrust and hate myself. How can I explain to you that, at the same time, I *do* distrust myself, that the world has succeeded, that I won't let this happen. I will not think what the world wants me to think. And that, in some way, my confession is a kind of subterfuge, a tactic, a way of overturning the damage at the root of its wounding. It is the silence that I fear more than anything, the pretense, the way it seems that, in the silence, suddenly some violence springs out that is unconnected. Is it better to keep things looking neat?

I realize upon coming home to my mother's house that nothing has changed. The anger is even more intense now. It's impossible to convince the abuser that they are wrong, that they should feel sorry for the victim. It's the pipe dream of a destroyed child that keeps surfacing into my fifties. So that when the conversation arrives about discipline, about hitting children, and I talk about the violence I felt as a child, my father's violence—how he beat me—my mother sits there, trying to be neutral. She never can.

She says, "Did you notice, Toi said, 'BEAT, BEAT,'" and she screws up her mouth to indicate with the most unpleasant emphasis that what I say is wrong. It's partly that she wants to spit, partly that she wants to scream, partly that she wants to say nothing, to sit back in her chair with her backbone right against the rung of the chair's spine.

I don't keep still. I can't. "Yes, BEAT is the word. When I was crawling along the floor trying to get away from him, begging, and he was beating me on the back of my legs and then when he continued to beat me until I stopped screaming, until I wiped every look of pain and sadness and anger off my face, beat me until my face was completely expressionless, I call that 'BEATING.' And when he'd carry me up four flights of stairs by my hair . . . yes, that was beating." I feel the muscles in my stomach harden and my body open so that I fit down into my anger like somebody who has the right, like Jesus throwing the tables over in the temple.

The next morning my mother meets me at the sink. I know something is wrong because I see the suffering on her face. "What's wrong?" I ask. At first she tries to stay "nice," controlled.

"Toi, I'm trying not to get into this, but here you go. You can never leave it alone." The point of reference for my mother is always eternity, what I've done to her my whole life.

"That look you looked at me last night, that look of hate, *Hate*," she says. "I hope as long as I live I'll never have somebody look at me like that again."

"Mother, I'm not going to be silent about this."

"Everybody's suffered," she says, "Everybody." And her face twists in personal outrage. "I've suffered terribly, and I'm still suffering," she says, "and I kept it to myself."

"But I was five years old," I say. "I needed your protection."

"You've been my judge and executioner," she screams. "All my life my judge and executioner."

"Mother, why is that you can have sympathy for everybody and everything in the world, every stray dog and cat"—she's very involved with the Humane Society—"but you can't see that I was hurt."

I'd like to let her off the hook, to stop talking about it, reliving it, and needing to be heard. I'd like to because she's suffered enough, I can tell by the way her anger strikes out at the men who do the lawn, the man at the video store, that deep inside she's more miserable than I. Maybe I am to blame. Maybe I am the worst person in the world and that's why my mother and father hurt me.

Later I say, "Maybe I better not go with you to the

store." And she says, "Why not go? Let's not carry our anger around."

I know she's trying hard to go past the things that separate us, and I am grateful because I don't want to be angry and hateful, so that I grab her and hold her tight. She seems frail, which makes me want to hold her protectively, and since she never lets me come close, I have to overcome the natural boundaries that she keeps between herself and the world in order to squeeze her, and I feel grateful, unafraid to tell her, "I love you, Mom. I'm not mad. In a way, I'm just a little two-year-old having a tantrum. I'm still your baby. I want your protection." If only she could want that part of me even now.

To my mother I will always be a threat. No matter how long I am "good," I will finally become "the other." When will the abuser understand the "life" under the skin of the thing abused?

Nothing is simple. At T.J. Maxx, when a homeless-looking man comes out of the dressing room—a man who may have the purplish blotches of someone with AIDS on his face—wearing a hat pulled down on his head, a black woman standing by the desk scrutinizes him with a look of cold assessment in her eyes that I have often seen in the eyes of black women. It is a stare disconnected, as if she has already made up her mind about what she is looking at and it is crazy and strange. There is a mild curiosity in her gaze that is so unashamed of getting caught that if the man were to look up and catch her interrogating him with her eyes, she'd probably roll her eyes at him as if *he* had done something wrong.

I admire that look, that look that is absolutely clear, that doesn't blanch, that is self-trusting. Clarity can be painful when someone looks at you that way, when someone is sure that it is *you* who are crazy. That look of self-assurance can't be argued with, even if you spend your whole life trying.

Sometimes black women have been known for a particular knack for self-protection, women who can think of something to say off the top of their heads that cuts to the quick, and they never even look back. One story was told about my gold-Cadillac Aunt Edith. When she finally got sick of the white woman in the cafeteria who always saved the ice cream for the white staff who taught at the school, she told her, "If I was a white woman who worked in a cafeteria, I'd commit suicide." She was known for her ability to see things only from her perspective, not to get confused by complications, to know what she wanted.

A part of me wishes that things could be so simple, that I could *not* see how and why the other is hurting, that I could withdraw into my own body, behind my own eyes and look out judgmentally. Don't I end up doing it anyway?

My mother used her enormous energy to set things right, to keep all the monthly bills and the exact amount to pay them neatly tucked in little brown envelopes held together with an old rubber band. Over the years, they became more tattered, a mark of my mother's austerity and loyalty, even to envelopes. Sometimes she stuck them in between the pages of *Your Pregnancy,* the book Dr. Milton had given her when she got pregnant. It was a soft-covered book with drawings of young white women my mother's age in long skirts, looking calm and pleasant. It detailed the unpleasantness of, for example, swollen ankles, in a kind of upbeat fashion. Of course I had to weigh the truth of that literature against the reports I had heard those Saturday mornings around our kitchen table about all the women who had almost died in pregnancy and labor. Many of the women had been the first black women in all-white hospitals. I wondered just how quickly the nurses put the instruments in their doctors' hands, how quickly they answered the women's call bells. They never mentioned race, perhaps because, having no other experience to compare this to, they took their treatment for granted. They blamed their suffering on their own bodies.

Once, my mother put me in my snow pants, sat me in the back of my wagon, and started off trudging through the snow tunnels of shoveled-back snow to the live-chicken market on Seven Mile. It was a walk of several miles. This was something that she hadn't yet tried in order to save her family money. There was a determination in her body like a soldier going into a bloody battle. On the trip home, the squawking chicken rode in a cage between my legs. I had some vague idea of what was to take place, though I believe I had already heard it said that my mother wasn't capable of doing it.

The chicken gleamed whitely in the basement, that place of thousand-leggers and a washing machine with a wringer that could wrench your arm off, where my mother went to do the despicable but necessary thing. I watched from a safe distance. She couldn't get hold of it correctly. It didn't make itself easy to kill. She had to fight with it as if she were fighting with a part of herself. Finally, she got the right grip and did it, and in some impossible way, the chicken got loose and ran around the basement pouring blood over everything. Maybe my mother was there in that basement a few months later, full-term, when she started to bleed, to lose the baby. All my life I have never been able to separate that blood in the basement, the chicken's, from my stillborn brother's.

She found time to earn a little extra money in the afternoons, while I was sleeping, by typing stencils at the metal kitchen table for the mailing department at Annis Furs, where my aunt was the manager. She'd put the big typewriter up on the kitchen table and put in the small cards that held a kind of ribbon paper that one could type on to make a stencil, which could then be used to stamp the same address over and over. In this way, thousands of pictures of fur coats were sent to the white suburbs of Detroit. I'd crawl around on the floor under her feet, becoming bored and pestering her to get her attention.

They had told my mother to stay off her feet, when she had toxemia, after the stillbirth, two times when she had TB, and when she had the hysterectomy, all before I was seven. But in some way, just like that chicken, she couldn't make herself behave. She had to get up. She'd pull the drapes closed and lie on the bed, trying to rest, trying to sleep, the way some people might try to lift up a refrigerator. It just couldn't be done.

Sometimes, when we'd go downtown on the bus, I'd get tired, but I'd always keep my head on her lap even if I went to sleep. I imagined that part of her just wanted to get off that bus and go on by herself. Even though another part couldn't imagine an existence in which we weren't connected.

My mother never got over the loss of her mother, who had died when she was eighteen. Her independent mother, Regina, had died of a stroke at forty-four while she was scrubbing a floor. She had been the head domestic for a rich Jewish family in Crowley,

Louisiana, the Kaplans, Rice King of the South, since my mother was three. Her mother had left her husband, the beautiful, "almost all-French," and delicate-boned Joe Baquet, in Beaumont, Texas, in that house in an alley with no address. Already one of her children had died: an infant, Bertram. The old woman who was baby-sitting tried to scrub away his chafed skin, the "crib cap," and scratched the fontanel. He developed an infection and died. A second boy, my grandmother's favorite and the most beautiful, Nalder, died at nine, crushed to death under a pile of lumber in a lumberyard where he was playing hide-and-seek. Colored children didn't have playgrounds in those days, my mother says in her own writing.

How did I learn these facts? It was my mother who passed on the stories of her life. We have learned to save even the most despicable evidence. The human mind wants to remember itself even more than it wants to forget, even more than it wants its own innocence. We want a record.

I read my poems about color to the incoming black graduate students. I start by chanting a song that had come to me during the middle of the night a few weeks ago—

> Beautiful faces,
> beautiful faces,
> beautiful faces,
> beautiful faces,
> beautiful faces,
> beautiful faces,
> beautiful faces,
> come in.

I sing it two times and, at the end, I point to my heart, singing, "come in." Then I ask them to sing it.

At first they are shy, they laugh at my request, mostly because they are surprised at my having asked them. It's best, when you surprise someone with your desire, to back off, to fill the space with words, so that they can think a little, all covered up by language. A yoga teacher told me that when your muscles start to feel strained, back up a little and talk to them, explain that they can relax, you won't hurt them, you'll take care of them, and then they'll open up and be trusting, so I start telling them the story of how this song came to me.

It happened after a reading that I had done in another city. When I had started reading, about fifty African-American students walked into the room all together—obviously they had come from a class with their teacher. I was so happy to see their faces—I don't often see fifty students of color together—that I stopped reading and said, "Come on up here and sit next to me with your beautiful faces."

At first I was talking to the young girls, for what is more beautiful than a group of young black girls, all different colors and sizes and degrees of composure, each with a certain sway?

And then I felt bad that I had left the boys out. But that only led me to understand that I wasn't just talking to the girls—even though I had thought I was. Because right at that moment, I started to say, "You beautiful-faced boys and girls, come right up here beside me," and they did! I could see that what I had thought had been a shorthand for what really was, I really had *seen!*

I didn't tell the group the whole story, but just enough for them to know that that song had come out of my recognition that what we carry inside is powerful and mysterious.

As I talked I could sense the room change slightly. It seemed to get a little warmer, and as if a little gold light had colored all of our faces.

And sure enough, we started to sing to ourselves and to each other. I asked them to look around the room at all of the faces, and I looked so unabashedly that I was afraid the men might think I was flirting. And perhaps I was. Perhaps one such as me who has kept love a secret for so long doesn't yet know how to refine its gestures.

Later, someone asked me if writing *The Black Notebooks* had helped me get better, and I talked about writing it in the middle of a terrible depression, being overwhelmed by feelings of shame. I said that by writing *The Black Notebooks*, I have come to realize that we negotiate a very complicated reality, and that we do the best we can, and that there is no perfect past to go back to. It is at this point of understanding that I think we develop compassion for ourselves and each other.

What haunts me about the evening was the harmony of our singing together, how, suddenly, not only did they sing, but the room erupted in Afro-Christian harmony, in the most beautiful church music I have ever heard. Something took over, so that I forgot my own song and stood amazed with my ears open. I was hollow and full. And when I sank down in my chair, they all stood up, still singing.

Acknowledgments

A manuscript written over twenty-five years owes grateful acknowledgment to so many people, not only close friends, but people whose names I don't know, people I met perhaps only once at a workshop or reading who told me that my words spoke for them. I especially want to acknowledge my family, friends, teachers, and editors, people whose presence spreads out over this time, and who encouraged the life this work came from.

I am grateful to my family: to my son, Anthony Derricotte, who went through a great many of the experiences chronicled in the book with me and kept humor and heart; to my grandson, Elliot Derricotte, and his mother, Camille, always in my corner; to my brother, Benjamin Webster, for his constant and protective love; and to my mother, Antonia Baquet, for her important contributions to the manuscript and for her wise counsel on matters both personal and professional. I am always grateful to my "sisters," those women in my family who are the sisters of my heart: Sylvia Hollowell (and her husband Melvin!); Bessie

Derricotte; the two Jeanne Derricottes; and Olivia Abner. I want to thank Bruce Derricotte, my anchor for thirty years, for never wavering in his faith in me and this work.

I am indebted to my teachers and mentors, the great lovers of truth and bravery, Galway Kinnell, Adrienne Rich, Lucille Clifton, Ruth Stone, and Pearl London.

I thank those friends and colleagues who read the manuscript at various stages in its development; their perceptive comments and arguments validated and inspired me: especially Madeline Tiger, who has been my most affirming, sensitive, and knowledgeable reader, and who has read and commented on this manuscript extensively and wisely at least ten times during the twenty years of our friendship; Nancy Zafris and Trudy Palmer, who helped show me a path when I thought there was nowhere to go; Joanne Braxton, who helped me to remember that life goes on after the writing, and whose fine editing eye helped sharpen the edges; and Mary Jane Krieger, my trusted secretary and friend. I am likewise indebted to Alicia Ostriker, Sharon Olds, Marilyn Hacker, Rita Dove, and Michelle Cliff for their own work, which leads me, and for the many times they encouraged me through doubt, and to Fiona Cheong, whose vision I have relied on so often at the end.

I am grateful for the sustaining friendship of Maxine Clair, Miriam DeCosta-Willis, Marilyn Mobley, Marita Golden, and Mary Helen Washington; for Joanne Gabbin and the wonderful women writers of Wintergreen; for my colleagues at Cave Canem; for Cornelius Eady and Sarah Michlem, Father Frances Gargani, Elizabeth Alexander, and Michael Weaver; for Anita Fellman, Jennifer Brody, and Patsy Sims; for my spiritual guides, Father Tom Hiney and Sister Sylvia Roselle.

I thank my editor, Jill Bialosky, for communication that leapt over impassable breaches; Charles Rowell, Naomi Long-Madgett, Ed Ochester, and Paul Coates for their love, hard work, and belief in our words made flesh. I thank Charlotte Sheedy and Neeti Madan for their readings and enthusiastic responses to the book.

I know I have inadvertently left out the names of those whose contributions were essential. Please forgive me. I beg you to know that I deeply value what you have given.